SPORTING PIGEON SHOOTING

MICHAEL BRANDER

A & C Black · London

To my shooting partners:
Andrew, Colin, David and Ian

Published by A & C Black (Publishers) Ltd.
35 Bedford Row, London WC1R 4JH

First published, 1986

Brander, Michael
  Sporting pigeon shooting.
  1. Pigeon shooting
  I. Title
  799.2'4865   SK325.P55

ISBN 0-7136-5528-3

Acknowledgements

My grateful thanks and acknowledgements are due to my
wife Evelyn, also to K.H.Grose and Michael Swan, for
undertaking the tedious task of reading and checking the
manuscript and proofs for mistakes. For any errors or
omissions, however, I am entirely responsible. My thanks
are also due to Kathleen Glass, Patrick Douglas-Hamilton
and Ian McCall for taking the photographs.

Front cover: Shooting wood pigeon in late August using a
straw bale hide. The gun is an over and under 20 gauge
and the ammunition a 13/14th oz (26 grm) load of no. 7 (2.4
mm) shot. (*Photo : Arthur Shepherd*)
Back cover: Part of a bag of over 100 wood pigeon shot over
decoys on a crop of winter oilseed rape. (*Photo : Arthur
Shepherd*)

CONTENTS

INTRODUCTION

Pigeons are birds which even keen shots tend to take for granted. They are so common in most parts of Britain that few people take the trouble to identify the various species, always assuming they know the differences. From the farmer's, or gardener's, viewpoint they are merely a pest, a feathered equivalent of the rabbit, which may also be shot throughout the year without a licence being required. Like the common cold they are seen as something which has always been with us, unchanged and unchanging over the centuries. The facts are rather different, for it only requires a steady change in our methods of farming, or a disease such as *myxomatosis,* and the pigeon might very quickly become comparatively rare.

The first book on pigeon shooting, entitled *Sport with Wood-pigeons*, by Max Baker, was published in 1934. It was then something of a revolutionary idea to write of pigeon shooting as a separate sport. His book, like the six or so which have appeared since, was primarily concerned with decoy shooting, then a comparatively new concept. It was to be several decades before pigeon shooting was accepted as a sport in its own right.

During the 'thirties and right up to the 'fifties, pigeon shooting was regarded as a somewhat nebulous 'poor man's sport' on the fringes of shooting, still mainly concerned with shooting over decoys. For the roughshooter, or game-shooter, the ever present rabbit provided the main background to their sport. Whenever they wished, in or out of season, they could be sure of an enjoyable day rabbit shooting. Then in the 1950s *myxomatosis* virtually wiped out rabbits for a decade or more. It is significant that some five more books on pigeon shooting were published in the late 'fifties and 'sixties as pigeon shooting began to take the place of rabbit shooting and at last became recognised as a sport in its own right, although the emphasis in many minds still remained on shooting over decoys.

During the 'sixties and 'seventies, while decoying could

still be obtained free from most farmers in return for crop protection, the pressures on the countryside were such that any form of shooting was increasingly eagerly sought, especially near large towns or cities. Where a barren downland shoot might previously have been taken for the rabbit shooting, now otherwise barren Forestry Commission shoots might be taken for the pigeon shooting. It was recognised by many game shots that an otherwise poor driven day might well be redeemed by an hour's flighting pigeons in to roost in the evening. At all levels of the shooting scale pigeon shooting was now recognised as a sporting form of shooting.

In the 'sixties and 'seventies the building of treetop level platform hides for flighting birds, as a feature well worth having on organised shoots, whether controlled by the owner, or a syndicate, also began to be more widely appreciated. The concept of shooting from cliff-, or quarry-top stands above the birds was still not so widely known. Then the 1981 Wildlife and Countryside Act altered the regulations concerning pigeon shooting as well as rightly removing the collared dove from the protected list.

As generally the most effective method of shooting large numbers, there is still an understandable tendency amongst conservative shooters, averse to change, to think only of shooting from hides over decoys and it is true that this can provide great sport. There are, however many types of decoy and many levels of hide. Shooting pigeons flighting in to roost can often provide great excitement and sport, as well as, on occasions, large bags, but anyone who has not shot from a platform hide at treetop level with birds coming from all angles, swerving and jinxing in the wind, cannot have appreciated the true potential of pigeon shooting. Then again, cliff- or quarry-top shooting, at pigeons flighting far below, can provide another sport altogether.

No matter how experienced a pigeon shooter may be on one level, he is likely to find that other levels present him with totally new angles on pigeon shooting. It will at least be a start if he takes a fresh look at his sport and the ground over which he shoots. If the shooting man, experienced or novice, is prepared to experiment he will find that pigeon shooting on various levels can provide extremely interesting and rewarding sport.

1

ORIGINS AND BACKGROUND

When did wood-pigeons first come to Britain?

The answer to this must be largely a matter of guesswork. Pleistocene fossil remains of wood-pigeons prior to the four Great Ice Ages have been found in Britain, but are very hard to date exactly. In any event the Ice Ages themselves must have radically altered the distribution of birds throughout Europe. The likeliest answer is that somewhere between 4000 and 3000 B.C., after the last Ice Age, wood-pigeons began to re-establish themselves in Britain. Living on a diet of grass seeds, beech nuts, acorns, berries and minute animal life such as wood-lice, but preyed on by wild-cats, pine-martens, hawks and corvids, to name only a few of the many predators with which they had to contend, they must have had a hard time to survive. The fact that they were re-established, despite the odds against them, indicates that they had already learned the all-important lesson of survival in the wild.

What is the difference between the stock-dove, and the rock-dove?

The stock-dove, *Columba oenas,* also known rather confusingly as the blue-rock, is a different species of pigeon from the rock-dove, *Columba livia.* There is some argument as to whether the domestic bird is descended from the rock-dove, or whether the rock-dove is merely the domestic bird gone wild, or feral, since they are the same species. As both the Greeks and Romans kept domesticated pigeons it may

1

be assumed that they were introduced to Britain by the Romans. Domesticated birds kept by the Saxons and the rock-dove living in the coastal cliffs were both well established before the arrival of the Normans almost a thousand years after the coming of the Romans. The stock-dove or blue-rock was by then also long established in inland areas suited to it.

What were the reasons for keeping domestic pigeons?

Domestic pigeons, also known confusingly at various times as stock-doves, were regarded as a useful culinary standby to provide a dish of fresh meat during the winter months when, apart from an occasional deer, gamebird or wildfowl, only salted meat was generally available. Like the fish pond and the rabbit warren, the dovecot played an important part in supplementing the winter food supplies of the aristocracy in their castles and manor houses or the clergy in their monasteries. Killing a domestic pigeon without permission was thus regarded as theft and punishable as such.

Although references to the pigeon in Britain from the Saxon period to the sixteenth century are minimal, according to a fourteenth century recipe it was generally eaten stuffed with garlic and herbs. It was also regarded by physicians in the Middle Ages as being of medicinal value and 'doves' applied to the soles of the feet were supposedly efficacious in cases of severe fever, even being used in this way in Scotland as late as the eighteenth century.

What was the attitude of sportsmen to wood-pigeons prior to the invention of the gun?

Although perhaps a not uncommon woodland bird, at least in most parts of Britain, by the early sixteenth century the wood-pigeon was not regarded as a sporting bird prior to, and indeed for a long time after, the invention of the gun. This is understandable enough since falconers would have been reluctant to use a gos-hawk, one of the wood-pigeon's principal predators, against them because of the danger of losing the hawk amongst the trees. A similar objection must have applied to flying a peregrine at rock-doves, for the chance of recovering a falcon at the foot of a cliff with a high tide running would have been remote. In general no falconer would risk months of training on a quarry so unworthy of the chase, which was equated in most minds with the humble domestic pigeon. Even the use of slings and cross-bow bolts must have seemed a pointless exercise when tame pigeons could be had with no effort. No doubt our ancestors, skilled with nets and traps, or 'engines' (later shortened to 'gins) must have occasionally caught wood-pigeons, stock-doves or rock-doves by liming, by netting, or by similar methods, but this was very clearly not considered worthy of mention. Taking into account the very large numbers of predators against which they had to contend it would have been surprising if any of the three species did much more than hold its own in scattered areas where the habitat part icularly favoured it.

When did the wood-pigeon become common throughout Britain?

This was a very slow process taking place over three centuries and reaching its climax in the nineteenth century as follows:

1. The sixteenth century saw the Reformation of the Church, the dissolution of the monasteries and the sweeping away of many of the old mediaeval ideas. There was the start of a gradual changeover from the mediaeval systems of open field farming grouped round the castle, or manor, to the enclosed pattern of fields and hedgerows we know today, providing an ideal habitat for the wood-pigeon. It was a process which was to last more than two centuries, and which greatly accelerated in the seventeenth and eighteenth centuries.

2. The Civil War in the seventeenth century led to the eventual breaking up of many estates and considerable anarchy at times. The large forests which had covered much of England had already been severely cut back as the demand for charcoal for ironworks had developed. With the growth of the Royal Navy the need for more and larger wooden ships increased and the forests suffered greater depredations. All this must inevitably have led to an improved habitat for the wood-pigeon and also to an increase in the number of feral pigeons as dovecots were left derelict beside despoiled monasteries or manor houses. There still remained, however, the ultimate controlling factor of numerous natural predators, which kept the overall population in check.

3. During the eighteenth century the pace of the enclosures quickened and spread northwards. The superiority of the new methods of farming being introduced was soon apparent, particularly to the squirearchy, who were also able to take full advantage of Acts of Parliament to establish their hold on the land. In addition the squires on their manors and the aristocracy on their estates were beginning to employ gamekeepers. Although their primary duty may have been to prevent poaching, they were also expected to rear some game and kill the predators—the hawks, corvids, martens, polecats, stoats, and weasels. These were, of course, also the enemies of the wood-pigeon. Thus, as early as 1775, in a book entitled *A Natural History of British Birds,* W. Hayes was the first to refer to wood-pigeons as being seen in considerable numbers, even if he was only referring to one specific area where all these factors were particularly favourable to them. He noted that wood-pigeons were:

'. . . *found in great abundance in Buckinghamshire, there being plenty of beech mast in that country of which they are exceedingly fond. In winter it is generally found in turnip fields, especially those bordering woods.*'

4. The explosion of the wood-pigeon population which took place in the first half of the nineteenth century in many

parts of England and Scotland came as a complete surprise to most people. A writer in the *Zoologist* in 1843 noted of the wood-pigeon in amazement: 'It was extremely rare in East Lothian about the end of the last century, where it now swarms to a most injurious extent.'

On the other hand Charles St John, that outstanding sportsman-naturalist, whose splendid book, chiefly about Morayshire, *Wild Sports of the Highlands,* still stands out as a classic work of a keen observer and gifted writer, wrote with considerable perception in 1845:

'Wood-pigeons . . . increase yearly in consequence of the destruction of their natural enemies . . . there are (also) considerable numbers of the little blue-rock pigeon breeding along the caves and rocks of the coast and feeding inland in great numbers.'

Why are pigeons not regarded legally as gamebirds?

The Game Laws were originally based on the old Forest Laws introduced by Canute and continued by the Normans. Altered under the Tudors to include the 'shooting of hayle shotte' they had become absurdly archaic and anachronistic by the nineteenth century. In the sixth edition of his famous book *Instructions to Young Sportsmen in all that relates to Guns and Shooting,* published just prior to the drastic revision of the Game Laws in 1831, which were based in part on his recommendations, Colonel Peter Hawker found little to say about pigeon shooting, but quoted an Act of James I regarding stock-doves, stating: 'Unless they are on your own property, or you are desired by the lawful owner to kill them, the penalty for shooting them is 20s...' He also noted, however, that: 'the owner of the land may kill such pigeons as he shall find devastating his corn.' When the 1831 Game Laws were passed, the law on pigeons, possibly at his suggestion, remained virtually unchanged. It was only thereafter that the full advantages of the pigeon as a sporting bird outside the Game Laws slowly began to be appreciated.

Why was pigeon shooting not more popular at any time?

There were three main reasons for this:

1. In the 1830s obtaining permission to shoot over land was easier in some respects, but more difficult in others. For a start, in a class-ridden society guns were supposedly only owned by freeholders and certainly anyone hoping for permission to shoot would have to be at least technically above suspicion of poaching.(From his own diaries, however, it is plain that despite his status as 'an officer and gentleman' Colonel Peter Hawker was all his life prepared to poach his neighbour's ground if he felt like doing so.) Of course in those days, prior to the introduction of the railways, access to the country was not as simple, but as strangers were rare, any visitor was likely to be received with great hospitality. A stranger had, however, to obtain permission to shoot from the landowner to ensure that no action for trespass might be taken against him. In short, then as now, the simple courtesies of life had to be observed. Then, as now, the landowner, or farmer, did not want people he did not know wandering over his land with a gun, but, then as now, it was a matter of concern to the farmers if pigeons were devastating newly sown, or laid, fields of grain, or greenstuffs. The landowner, even if he reared partridges and pheasants, could not prevent the farmer protecting his crops and no doubt many yeoman farmers enjoyed their sport as a result. There is indeed at least one drinking song penned about this date on pigeon shooting, which extols the advantages of not requiring a game licence and which, no doubt, was sung lustily at farming dinners by yeoman farmers who took full advantage of the law.

2. One particular form of pigeon shooting which developed as a popular pastime from the late eighteenth century onwards had gradually turned public opinion against all forms of the sport. This was competitive shooting at live birds released from traps. This so-called sport, likened by Colonel Hawker to badger-baiting, was run on much the

same lines as the modern sport of clay-pigeon shooting, its successor. Specially bred domestic pigeons were released from traps placed in a semi-circle in front of the waiting gun in the centre. The first club to practise this form of sport was formed in 1777. In 1823, after being criticised for using guns of enormous proportions, members were forced to limit the size of the guns allowed at their pigeon shoots. One champion shot used a gun with a muzzle diameter of an inch and a half. Since a four bore only has a muzzle diameter of .948 this justified the contemporary criticism that: 'he may as well carry a field piece as the gun with which he usually shoots his pigeon matches.' It was this sort of dubious tactic, inspired more by the considerable stake money and side-bets involved rather than the question of cruelty, which brought competitive shooting into growing disrepute. Public feeling against the shooting of live pigeons grew in volume from the 1820s until by 1900 it had reached a considerable pitch. Nevertheless, it was not until 1910 that live pigeon shooting was finally made illegal in Britain. (It has since gradually become illegal elsewhere throughout the world and is now only carried on legally in Italy, South America and Mexico, where the stakes are still very high.)

3. The agricultural depression of the 1870s and '80s, caused by the uncontrolled imports of corn from the Mid-West States of America, frozen butter and mutton from New Zealand and frozen beef from the Argentine, no longer made farming economic and, until the 1914-18 War saw a brief revival, many farms earned more from their shooting rents than from the crops or livestock they produced. Most shooting tenants were, of course, more interested in shooting game than pigeons, which were regarded as one of the farmer's or farmworker's perquisites. With the introduction of the breechloading double-barrelled gun in the mid-nineteenth century many old guns were passed on to farm workers and cottagers so that by the end of the century almost everyone in the country had some sort of gun. Pigeons were regarded as

the poor man's quarry and were mostly shot by countrymen for the pot, or to protect growing crops rather than for sport. With intensive keepering killing off their predators the wood-pigeon population had probably greatly increased, but since farming was uneconomic anyway it was not seen as a particular pest.

How did the First World War of 1914-1918 affect matters?

During the U-boat blockade of Britain in the 1914-18 War the importance of farming was very quickly appreciated. The desirability of keeping wood-pigeons under control became a matter of governmental concern for the first time. The Ministry of Agriculture issued directives to farmers and landowners, but little beyond this was achieved. Almost as soon as the war was over, agriculture, faced with uncontrolled overseas competition again, became once more a depressed industry. As in the latter part of the nineteenth century and the Edwardian era, shooting rents were often greater than the returns that could be earned from the land. In addition many large estates had been sold and split up into smaller areas because of increased death duties. On the whole the pigeon flourished unchecked, but was still regarded as the countryman's perquisite rather than of interest to the gameshooter.

What were the effects of the Second World War of 1939-45?

Once more farming became all-important as another U-boat blockade tightened its grip. Again the Ministry of Agriculture issued directives and little else. Because of a scarcity of cartridges, more woods being felled and increased land under the plough providing an ideal pigeon habitat, the war years probably saw a considerable increase in the wood-pigeon population. After the war, when farming remained economically of the highest importance the Ministry of Agriculture was eventually forced to take action. Even so it was only in 1954, nearly ten years after the end of the war, following the sort of delay which could only have been tolerated in a bureaucratic organisation, that the Ministry finally stopped issuing edicts and instead started issuing subsidised cartridges to *bona fide* shots with really very little more success. They did, however, about the same time sponsor a field research project under the aegis of a biologist, Dr R.K.Murton, which was to have a very considerable effect in the 1960s.

What was the attitude to wood-pigeon shooting in the 1950s?

There were several viewpoints:
1. With the advent of subsidised cartridges many people qualified willingly enough as *bona fide* shots by approaching the local pest control officer and applying to join in occasional organised shoots. With a large proportion of their cartridges paid for there was a considerable tendency to blaze away indiscriminately. Very few of these organised shoots produced worthwhile results, but on the whole most people enjoyed them, even if this was not strictly the point of the proceedings.
2. The average keen game shot probably began to take a greater interest in pigeon shooting because of the increasingly high costs of rearing game. Furthermore, the advent of *myxomatosis* in the early 1950s meant that for a decade, or more, the rabbit was no longer available to swell the bag on the roughshoot, or to help to pay the keeper's wages on a keepered shoot. With the additional hazard of poisonous seed dressings causing deaths and sterility in gamebirds, the wood-pigeon assumed a fresh importance.
3. It was still widely thought that the wood-pigeon migrated in the winter months from Scandinavia and the Continent. Large flocks of slightly smaller and darker birds

were seen on the south and east coasts in the winter months and it was held that these were foreign birds migrating from Norway or France. They were of course, as is now appreciated, merely young birds not yet fully marked. Although there may at times be some two-way migration between Europe and Britain, there is not a large wood-pigeon population in Norway.

What were the results of Dr R.K.Murton's researches?

After six years' field research sponsored by the Ministry of Agriculture Dr R.K.Murton produced statistics in the early 1960s which showed apparently conclusively that pigeon shooting does little or nothing to control their numbers. He concluded that 70% of all young wood-pigeons left their nests in August and September, so that by October the wood-pigeon population was virtually doubled. He estimated that there were an average of 63 birds per hundred acres in July, rising to 154 in September and returning to around 70 in February following the inevitable mortality from lack of feeding in the winter. His conclusion was that shooting had little or no effect on numbers since the birds would in any event die from lack of nutrition. Not surprisingly there was considerable dispute about the validity of his findings and an outcry in the popular sporting Press, but this did not stop the Ministry accepting them and phasing out the cartridge subsidy in 1969.

What was the situation in the 1970s?

There was an intensification of the trends in the 1950s and 1960s, resulting in a knock-on effect:
1. Between the late 1950s and mid-1960s there were no fewer than four books written on pigeon shooting, which probably reflected accurately the increasing interest of the average shooting man in this aspect of his sport in the 1970s.

2. In the early 1970s, when the burning of stubbles was first introduced, there was a noticeable decrease in the numbers of wood-pigeons in some areas. This was thought by some to have been caused by over-shooting, but Dr R.K.Murton's theory was that this had nothing to do with it. He argued that earlier burning of the stubbles and improved harvesting techniques left less grain for the birds after harvest. Taking into account also the introduction of earlier ploughing, he maintained it was merely the natural effect of lack of feeding which was causing a shortage of birds. He argued convincingly that shooting would make no difference. Large-scale uprooting of hedges was also creating a prairie countryside in parts of East Anglia, altering the habitat and causing wood-pigeons in these areas to alter their habits.

3. There were several reasons for the increasing interest in pigeon shooting, but chief amongst them was probably the fact that every year since the war several thousand more acres of erstwhile farmland have been swallowed up by concrete, for factories, housing estates, new towns, new motorways, airfields, rocket launching sites and similar essentials of modern civilisation. As one consequence, game shooting has been steadily growing more and more difficult to obtain and more expensive. Accordingly this increased the pressure on pigeon shooting and there is nothing like scarcity to raise values and increase demand.

4. The constantly increasing expenses of shooting, of rearing game, and of keepering ground, as well as the pressures on the economy as a whole, made more and more landowners and shooting syndicates cost-conscious and forced them to look for every way to get the most from their shooting. Increasingly they began to appreciate the importance of pigeon shooting and it was generally realised that in its various forms and at several levels it can provide good sport throughout the year.

5. While most game shots were aware that flighting pigeons in to roost at the end of the day could often provide the best part of the day's sport this was sometimes no

longer enough to satisfy them. After their introduction to shooting from platform hides, at treetop level, or above, increasing numbers of landowners and shots appreciated what sport they had been missing in the past. At all levels pigeon shooting had at last graduated from being merely ancillary to game shooting to being a sport in its own right.

What effect did the 1981 Wildlife and Countryside Act have on pigeon shooting?

The stock-dove, *Columba oenas,* was put on the protected list, as was the rock-dove, *Columba livia,* now only to be found in Caithness and Sutherland. The latter have suffered from the effects of domestic escapees mating with them and producing feral crosses. On the other hand, quite rightly, the collared dove, *Stretopelia decoacto,* which has spread widely since its colonisation in the 1950s was removed from the protected list and may now be shot throughout the year. Feral birds, listed in the Act as *Columba livia,* may also be shot throughout the year wherever found, whether in quarries, cliffs, or farm buildings, subject, of course, to the permission of the landowner.

2

Varieties: Habits and Habitat

Throughout the world there are approaching 300 species of pigeons, or doves. (The use of either term is correct.) The exact number is open to argument, but there is no doubt that they provide more sport than any other single species of bird or beast. Although many of these species of pigeon appear able to withstand unlimited shooting, there are others which need to be protected. It is worth noting for instance that five species of pigeons are already listed amongst the extinct species of the world, including the now almost legendary ground-nesting dodo and the once immensely numerous passenger pigeon.

As late as the mid-nineteenth century the passenger pigeon was still considered one of the commonest birds in North America, the flocks being described by Audubon as seemingly limitless. It was rendered extinct by a complete absence of any control over its annual ruthless slaughter for commercial purposes and by the totally reckless destruction of its natural habitat. These two factors combined to make a once numerous species of pigeon extinct within a period of some fifty years. The last passenger pigeon died in 1914 and that sad fact should remain an object lesson to us today. Even the seemingly ubiquitous wood-pigeon could disappear if we continue to root out hedges and copses, thus destroying its natural habitat.

Columba palumbus (ring-necked dove)

In Britain there are only five species of pigeons, or doves, which are likely to be encountered. Of these the most important and by far the commonest is the wood-pigeon, *Columba palumbus,* also known as the ring-necked dove, ring-dove, ring-neck, or, more familiarly, as the woodie. In Scotland it is also known as the cushat, or cushie doo, and in Wales as the quist, or queest. It is a well known, easily recognised, handsome, heavily built, well feathered bird, weighing about 1-1½lbs and measuring about 16 inches in length, with blue grey upper parts, a noticeable white patch on either side of the neck, white bands across the wing and another broad white band across the underside of the tail. Both this and the wing bands are very prominent in flight, as are the white patches on the side of the neck. It has reddy-pink legs and a yellow bill with a noticeable white lump above the nostrils. The eye is light coloured and bright, giving the bird a well-earned reputation for alertness.

The wood-pigeon is a greedy feeder with an unfortunate liking for most agricultural crops, particularly corn and freshly sown cereals and clover, also such green food as kale, brussels sprouts, cabbages, broccoli and peas. The wood-pigeon's beak is well adapted for tearing the leaves of vegetation and it will devour a considerable amount of food in a day. It also has the advantage that it can retain food in its crop to digest later. It will normally fill its crop in the morning and spend the middle part of the day digesting its food before feeding again in the afternoon. During the short winter days it will stuff its crop to the maximum before flighting back to roost to digest it at its leisure.

More than 1200 wheat grains have been taken from the crop of a single bird and, as many keepers and experienced pigeon shots know, it is quite possible where pigeons are shot regularly to feed a small flock of hens from the crops of the birds shot around harvest time. It is also quite common when shooting birds flighting back to roost in winter for their crops to burst on hitting the ground, so heavily have they stuffed themselves with the green stuff on which they have been feeding. It is only fair to add that they will as cheerfully gorge themselves when they can on acorns, beechnuts, hawthorn and elderberries. They will also eat any small insects, such as woodlice, tiny snails, or worms, which they come across while feeding. From the countryman's viewpoint, their worst feature is that they will wreak havoc on crops of many kinds on farms, smallholdings, allotments, or kitchen gardens, from the stage of sowing right through to the harvest. It is because of this unfortunate propensity that the wood-pigeon is rightly regarded as a pest by every farmer, smallholder and gardener.

A rough diet sheet of the wood-pigeon's favourite foods month by month throughout the year might run something as follows. In January and February, clover, tops of green crops, brassica, weeds, thorn and other berries. March and April would see a changeover to sowings of clover, corn, peas and beans, as well as weeds and early shoots. In May and June the wood-pigeon is probably concerned principally with weeds, clover, peas, oil seed rape and garden crops. July and August are the months mainly concerned with corn, peas, oil seed rape, weeds, and small snails or other insects, or minute animal life. September and October are in the main chiefly spent gleaning the stubbles, searching for newly drilled crops and in the woods and hedgerows for berries. November and December are generally spent in the woods and hedgerows, feeding on hips, haws, beech mast and acorns, or on kale and the tops of green crops, also on various remaining weeds.

There is a natural tendency for wood-pigeons to be found in greater quantities in those areas providing what to them is a thoroughly satisfactory habitat with plenty of arable land interspersed with regular plantations, small copses, or tree-grown hedgerows, which provide plentiful nesting cover combined with many suitable areas for feeding. East

Anglia, except where prairie farming has taken over, and the intensively farmed east coast areas, the Lothians and Angus in Scotland, as far as Morayshire in particular, provide just such suitable ground, as do considerable areas of Kent, Sussex, Hampshire and Oxfordshire, extending into parts of Wiltshire and Dorset. Not surprisingly, such favoured areas have a very noticeably larger wood-pigeon population compared with other parts of the country where the same happy mixture of a suitable feeding area side by side with a convenient nesting ground is not widely available.

Wood-pigeons will, nevertheless, nest in all sorts of places and the nests are sometimes surprisingly low, even being found on the ground in treeless areas. They prefer to nest, however, in hedges, bushes, or trees, generally about ten feet or more above ground. Conifers on the edges of plantations surrounding arable ground are a favoured place, being close by a convenient source of food. The nests themselves are usually clumsy affairs, little more than a platform of twigs and not difficult to find. They are merely large enough to support the adult birds and the two long white eggs which are the normal clutch laid.

While the offspring of each mating is thus limited to two, the incubation period is only seventeen days and the wood-pigeon compensates by laying an average of five clutches a year. Although they have been known to nest in almost every month of the year, given a good spell of weather, the highest percentage of young to hatch successfully is undoubtedly during the months of July and August. Then, of course, the harvest provides a readily available and plentiful supply of food.

It appears from the research conducted under the supervision of Dr R.K.Murton that March marks the normal start of the annual breeding cycle and October the end, but there are always exceptions to every rule. Furthermore, there must be something approaching a month's difference in the breeding cycle between wood-pigeons in, for instance, Aberdeenshire at one end of

Britain and Kent, or Dorset, at the other. Then again, variations in the weather from one year to another may cause annual fluctuations throughout the country. Admittedly the formal courtship behaviour, the bowing of the head and raised tail display of the male bird, the distinctive coo-ing mating call and the mutual preening and billing of the mated pair, as well as the typical swooping display flight accompanied by a sharp clap of the wings are most frequently observed from March to October, but any countryman with an interest in birds must have noticed numerous exceptions. Any young born in the winter months, of course, are almost certainly bound to die from predation, or else starvation. It is indeed the high incidence of egg stealing and mortality of the chicks in the months when there is little leaf to provide cover or sufficient food available, which together prevent the otherwise almost inevitable wood-pigeon population explosion.

Throughout the spring and summer months it is common to find the eggs of wood-pigeons lying on the ground as mute evidence of a successful attack on a nest. Jays, magpies, jackdaws, rooks and crows will leave evidence of their depredations in the shape of the empty eggshell with a small round hole in it. Squirrels, or rats, leave a larger jagged hole at the base of the egg and stoats, or weasels, will leave two small teeth marks. Only when the remains of the egg show the unmistakeable chip marks all round, as if the top had been cleanly sliced off with a knife, can it be certain that the chick has at least been hatched. Although such an empty shell may be found beneath the nest it is very often carried some distance away by the parent birds, or by the wind.

The eggs are incubated by the female with the male bird taking his turn twice daily, but if either bird is killed the indications are that the other will carry on alone and hatch the young. The chicks are known as squabs and are somewhat repulsive to look at, with a soft, grey, flattish beak and wrinkled blue-grey skin very thinly covered with a yellow hairy down. In the early stages, that is for the first week or so, they are fed by the parent birds regurgitating a creamy, cheesy substance known correctly as crop milk, although perhaps more frequently referred to as pigeon's milk. This is gradually mixed with whatever feed is generally available at that time and thus the young birds are introduced by degrees to their natural diet.

Within about ten days the squab's yellow down has begun to be replaced by the first juvenile feathers, and the soft beak, useful for obtaining crop milk, has begun to take on the adult shape. As soon as this stage is reached the squabs also develop a defence mechanism which they employ against any intruder to the nest. They will puff up their crop by filling it with air, like a toad, or bull frog swelling itself up, then spreading their wings, they will lunge forward to peck with a hissing sound. They can give even a human a surprisingly hard peck and no doubt this performance will generally be enough to frighten off any of the less determined predators. The fact remains, however, that despite this surprisingly pugnacious defence mechanism the squabs are ready enough prey for any hunting cat, or bloodthirsty stoat, weasel, or rat. Owls, hawks and corvids are also likely predators. At this stage the squab is still extremely vulnerable to attack, more especially, of course, when the nest is in an exposed position, or when there is no concealing leafy growth to hide it from view.

After a month the squabs are generally ready to leave the nest, although still awkward and clumsy. Their first juvenile plumage is duller and greyer than that of the adult birds, lacking the white markings on either side of the neck. At around six weeks they will start their first moult, but this may be halted during the winter months so that it is not fully completed until the following spring. It is at this intermediate stage between leaving the nest and their first adult moult that the young pigeons are again very vulnerable to attack by sparrow-hawks, cats and similar powerful, determined predators, but within a few weeks they have gained most of the adult's cunning and alertness.

There is some evidence that during the winter months, particularly in the November/December period, there may be a degree of migration by wood-pigeons. Stories of large numbers of foreign birds arriving in the United Kingdom, either on the shores of Norfolk, Yorkshire, or Berwickshire have usually related to movements within the U.K. and the smaller, darker-coloured birds have merely been young wood-pigeons still in juvenile plumage. Nevertheless, it is clear that on occasions there are mass migrations, both to and from Europe, which have been observed. On the other hand insufficient is known about these migrations, or mass pigeon movements, to be clear exactly what causes them, or when and where they may be expected. It would appear from what little reliable recorded evidence there is available that, at least in the initial stages, they are generally prompted by a search for food.

There can be little doubt that the tendency for southerly movements of large flocks of wood-pigeons, which has often been noted during the November/December months, has its origins in their gregarious habits. In the winter months especially this gregariousness, or flock instinct, of the wood-pigeon is its most noticeable feature. At this time they will both feed and roost, young and old birds together, in a flock often amounting to several hundred. Where roosting woods are not readily available they may fly several miles to a communal roost accommodating as many as two or three thousand birds. Inevitably when congregating in such numbers they are liable to be affected by a tendency to mass movements.

Even during the breeding season from March to October the same gregarious instincts are noticeable when feeding. A single wood-pigeon flying past a flock of feeding birds will almost invariably swoop down to join them. A flock of wood-pigeons feeding in a field will also be seen to move round the field as a group, rather than spread out feeding by themselves and scattered around the entire area. The birds in the rear will occasionally fly over the heads of those in front and take the lead, to be replaced in their turn in due course. Any birds feeding apart will soon join the main body. Thus they move across the ground in a surprisingly orderly way and the damage done to the crops on which they are feeding is very much more concentrated.

The movement of the white neck-patches bobbing up and down as the birds feed, or the flash of the white wing-bars as a pigeon alights, or flies over the heads of the flock to a fresh feeding point, serve as a beckoning signal to attract the attention of any passing wood-pigeons. These may circle round before flighting in to join the feeding birds, but they will sometimes almost fall out of the sky with a peculiar tumbling flight in their haste to join the flock on the ground. When alerted to any danger the feeding birds automatically raise their heads at once so that their white patches immediately become invisible. At this warning sign any approaching bird will immediately jinx away.

Contrary to popular opinion the wood-pigeon's eyesight is not as good as that of many other birds. Although it is quick to observe movement and wary of strange objects, its peripheral vision is distinctly poor. Nor is its hearing as good as is sometimes believed. It is usually, however, alert to the sound of any predator approaching, especially man. Perhaps the commonest sound to be heard on many woodland walks is the familiar clatter of wings and the snapping of small twigs as a wood-pigeon departs from a tree, or bush, on the opposite side to the line of approach. The sound of one bird departing is enough to alert the next-in-line and so on. They are almost invariably careful, however, to keep a hedgerow, or line of trees, between themselves and whoever is approaching, until safely out of gunshot.

Columba oenas (stock-dove)

Apart from feral birds, domestic escapees that have mated in the wild and which are now probably one of the largest groups, the next commonest pigeon is the stock-dove, *Columba oenas*, also widely known as the blue rock. It is found throughout the United Kingdom, but in far lesser numbers than the wood-pigeon, although the two species, along with feral birds, intermingle freely on occasions. Only about 13 inches long, it has no white on its neck or wings, but has two broken black wing bars. An overall darker blue-grey colour than the wood-pigeon, it can be seen at close quarters to have a handsome glossy green patch on either side of the neck, while the throat and breast are a pinkish-mauve. In flight it has a noticeably faster wing-beat than the wood-pigeon and also, being smaller, gives the illusion of being a dumpier, less streamlined, bird. The stock-dove has a softer and shorter coo-ing call note than the rather hoarser and more prolonged call of the wood-pigeon.

A major point of difference between the stock-dove and the wood-pigeon, not apparent at first glance, is the shape and size of their beaks. The stock-dove's beak is slightly shorter and less powerful, more adapted for eating weed-seeds, which constitute the major part of its diet, than for tearing vegetation. Although the stock-dove will eat grain freely at harvest time and is usually the first to find newly sown fields of grain, it is even then more often content merely with weed seeds. The diets of the two species are thus complementary rather than in competition with one another.

Perhaps owing to the difference in eating habits the stock-dove tends to move rather faster than the wood-pigeon when feeding. The stock-dove is also more wary in that it tends to flight into the middle of fields, rather than close to the edges. Although its courting habits, including courting flights, are very similar to those of the wood-pigeon and it may be found nesting in exactly the same sort of places, the stock-dove is extremely adaptable and will also nest in the hollows of trees, in quarries, cliffs, or farm buildings. In general it may be regarded as less harmful than the wood-pigeon, yet during the winter months it generally succeeds in maintaining itself in markedly better condition than the larger bird. The stock-dove is protected under the 1981 Wildlife and Countryside Act, but if a farmer, or landowner, considers they are harming crops it seems he can apply to the local authority for permission to shoot them.

Columba livia (rock-dove)

Very similar in size to the stock-dove is the rock-dove, *Columba livia,* which is distinguished by a lighter-coloured back, two very clearly marked black wing bars and a noticeable white rump patch. It has similar glossy green neck markings to the stock-dove, but the throat and breast are grey. The beak is minimally stronger than that of the stock-dove, but basically the two have similar tastes in food. It is possibly due to their similar, and therefore competitive feeding habits that, although the stock-dove population has remained fairly constant in many areas, the rock-dove's numbers have been steadily declining over the past hundred years. As the name implies, the rock-dove is found in cliffs and quarries near to the coast. When disturbed it normally flies extremely sharply downwards, where the influence of the wind currents blowing against the cliffs generally results in a highly erratic, swerving flight. It will roost on ledges, or in caves in the rocks, and feeds inland.

Because of the difficulty of access and its highly erratic flight, the rock-dove has never been widely shot. Although either the ancestor or, less probably, the descendant of the domesticated birds kept in castles, monasteries and manors during the Middle Ages to augment winter supplies of fresh meat, the true rock-dove is now no longer found except in the cliffs of Caithness and further north and west in the highlands of Scotland, where squabs and eggs have been frequently sought by keen pigeon breeders to supply them with fresh blood. The main reason for the decline in numbers, however, is probably that, over the years, numerous feral escapees from domestic dovecots have inter-bred with them, producing new strains of feral birds which in most areas have submerged almost all traces of the true wild species. The rock-dove is now, understandably, included as a protected bird under the 1981 Wildlife and Countryside Act, but again it would seem that if a crofter, or farmer, in Caithness felt his crops were being threatened by flocks of rock-doves he would be entitled to apply to his local authority for permission to shoot them.

Streptopelia turtur (turtle-dove) and Streptopelia decoacta (collared dove)

The only two other doves likely to be encountered are the turtle-dove, *Streptopelia turtur,* a summer migrant, which is protected, and the somewhat similar collared dove, *Streptopelia decoacto,* which may be shot. Each of these is markedly smaller than any of the other species, being only some 11 inches long. The turtle-dove has brownish wings and a noticeably black tail with white edges. It has a soft almost sleepy call and is generally found in open bushy country, or orchards, but is not common in Scotland.

The collared dove, although a comparative newcomer, having only reached the U.K. in 1952, has spread throughout the country and is still increasing steadily in numbers, especially in Southern Scotland. It has a narrow black half-collar round the back of its neck. The upper parts are dusty brown with pale blue grey shoulders, and it has red eyes. It has a characteristic short, rather harsh and unpleasing flight call. It prefers to nest in trees, usually around ten or fifteen feet above ground and is frequently found close to villages, or buildings.

An interesting point is that in crosses between the two species the result is almost indistinguishable from the collared dove, so that in course of time the turtle-dove is likely to suffer the same fate as the rock-dove. The collared dove shows every sign of becoming a pest and is listed by the 1981 Wildlife and Countryside Act as being a bird which may be shot by authorised persons at all times. Apparently it may not be sold, but it should still be shot whenever the opportunity arises and although small it is good to eat.

Amongst the birds listed by the Wildlife and Countryside Act of 1981 that may be shot by authorised persons at all times and, when shot, sold at all times, are wood-pigeons, listed as *Columba palumba*, also feral pigeons, listed under *Columba livia* the latin name for the rock-dove. As indicated, however, feral escapees have largely swamped the true *Columba livia*, or rock-dove, for inevitably each year, without undue carelessness on their part, local pigeon breeders throughout the country, whether breeding for show or racing, lose a number of their birds to the wild. These escapees crossing with the original rock-dove, or other pigeons gone feral, can sometimes produce extremely interesting results. Exotics such as Birmingham Rollers, West of England Flying Tumblers, or Flying Tipplers are bound to add interest to the local stocks of wild pigeons, whether nesting in quarry faces, in cliff crannies, or in farmyards, or simply frequenting the rooftops and streets of the nearest town or village, and living off the local gardens and allotments.

There is little need to wonder why these highly bred birds tend to overshadow the native birds. It is sufficient to know that blue and red chequer matings will produce mealy, or red cocks and blue or blue chequer, hens. Thus, when such interesting crosses as mealy hens, dark chequer cocks, blue whites, opal mosaics, mealy pieds and others escape into the wild, there are clearly many varieties of bird which may be encountered as a result. It is certainly not uncommon to see many startlingly varied birds with highly exotic colouring when shooting in quarries, or on cliffs, or close to towns, villages, or farmyards. On the whole, however, such feral birds are generally fairly easily distinguished from domestic birds through being in the company of other wild birds, even sometimes seemingly recognisable rock-doves, rather than among a flock of homers, or racing pigeons. It is, however, very easily understandable how the native pigeons have become submerged amongst these varied highly bred species gone wild.

It is, of course, rightly illegal knowingly to shoot racing pigeons and a considerable fine (£250) may be incurred for so doing. Quite apart from any possible fine, no sportsman would ever knowingly interfere with someone else's enjoyment in this way. In general, however, it is unlikely that racing pigeons will be encountered when decoying wood-pigeons, or flighting wild birds coming in to roost, but there are rare occasions when a racing pigeon is shot accidentally. Such a bird is easily identified by the presence of a ring on its legs with the date of registration and the breeder's number as the permanent evidence of identity. This should be removed and returned to the police, or the nearest known pigeon breeder, who will see that the owner is duly informed of the loss of his bird.

Breeding pigeons, like any other hobby, can be a costly business and the price of first-rate birds can easily run into three figures, or even higher. A bird which has gone astray for any length of time, say several weeks or more, is generally no loss, but one killed while competing in a race, especially when possibly in a winning position, may represent a very heavy loss, as much for its breeding potential as any prize money involved, although that may be considerable. From a breeder's viewpoint it is usually desirable to learn of the demise of a bird since this provides useful, even if possibly negative, information as to future breeding plans, but the pigeon shooter must always be on the alert to avoid any possible mistakes.

3

Initial Requirements

Shooting

To write on obtaining pigeon shooting as if everyone was
similarly placed is clearly an absurdity. The individual who
lives and works in a large city with no friends in the
country has very different problems when it comes to
looking for pigeon shooting from the person who lives and
works in a small country town. Equally obviously the large
landowner with varied shooting at his command will have
different views on pigeon shooting from a farmworker on
a neighbouring farm. Each has differing requirements and
each may be interested in a different form of sporting
pigeon shooting, yet each on their various levels may enjoy
good sport, and who is to say at the end of the day whose
enjoyment has been the greatest?

The individual to whom money is no object, who is not
prepared, or is unable, to spend the time and trouble to
go out and look for shooting, will, of course, obtain it
through an agent, or advertisement, easily enough, but
he will pay an inflated price for it. The individual who is
on a tight budget but is prepared to take his time finding
the sort of shooting he wants may end up not only paying
a great deal less, if indeed anything at all, but enjoying
better sport. In sport as in much else there is generally
a close correlation between effort expended and satisfaction
achieved.

There is no doubt, however, that the city dweller with
no friends in the country faces a considerable problem in
obtaining pigeon shooting. His first step, if he does not
know how to handle a gun safely or shoot reasonably

accurately, should be to go to a gunsmith, explain his intentions, hire, or buy, a gun and take lessons on gun handling and shooting at the nearest shooting school. It may be that he will meet people in the course of these proceedings who will help him to obtain shooting, but even so he would do well to read the subject up in his local library. He should also read the various sporting journals and in these he will find the names and addresses of the nearest pigeon shooting, or wildfowling clubs, to which he can apply for membership. These are usually, but not always, affiliated to the British Association for Shooting and Conservation, BASC, so that another course open to him is to write to their headquarters.(Marford Mill, Rossett, Wrexham, Clwyd, LL12 0HL.)

The only pitfall in this plan is that many of these local clubs have a limited membership and may also have quite a long waiting list. Another snag for the inexperienced shot is that the club secretary is sure to enquire as to the prospective member's experience. No club will wish to enroll a lunatic member who may let them down by failing to follow the simple code of country behaviour, by for instance leaving gates open, or litter lying around, including empty cartridge cases, by trampling through growing crops, parking cars in gateways, bringing along uncontrolled dogs and uninvited friends, shooting dangerously close to stock or people, poaching game, or the numerous other crimes of omission or commission. Even the most expert of shots will not be welcome if he behaves in this way.

It is thus possible that our aspiring pigeon shooter finds himself in a chicken and egg situation, since he seemingly cannnot gain experience without joining a club and yet without experience most clubs are reluctant to enroll him. In such a situation, or if the city- or town-based aspirant finds no clubs available in the locality he favours, he might do worse than advertise in a suitable local paper for similar minded people. He may then be in a position to form a partnership with two or three others, or a syndicate of six or seven, or even start his own small club with the advantage of having a say in its control.

In any of these cases there should also be less of a problem in obtaining pigeon shooting since there will be more people looking for it. Furthermore to some extent a farmer is probably more likely to listen sympathetically to an approach from a partnership, syndicate, or club, rather than an individual, more especially if the point is made that he may rely on them to produce guns to shoot pigeons on his land whenever he sees his crops being damaged. The valid point can also be made that anyone misbehaving in any way loses his membership of the partnership, syndicate, or club, at once. While it may be necessary and tactful to offer to pay for the privilege, it could well be that they are offered the pigeon shooting free in return for their services when required.

In these circumstances, of course, the pigeon shooters concerned will have to turn out whenever necessary throughout the year to protect the crops. Despite this sometimes onerous obligation, which must be honoured if they wish to keep their free shooting, they may well obtain as good sport as any. Everything depends on the relationship they achieve with the farmer or farmers concerned, for with the growing pressures on the countryside and the steadily increasing gap between country and town, the farmer and the countryman is ever more chary of having strangers he does not know, or is not sure he can trust, on his land, whether or not they offer to pay a good rent for game or pigeon shooting.

It may be, however, that the city- or town-dwelling prospective pigeon shooter does not wish to join a club or syndicate, and who shall blame him if he prefers to go it alone? Presuming that, at any rate initially, he is prepared to pay for his sport, there is little problem involved. His first goal is to gain experience and he will find numerous advertisements in the shooting journals or farmhouse holiday brochures, offering shooting of various kinds for long or short periods, often with offers of tuition included for the novice gun. If he is prepared to devote a week or two of his holiday to his chosen sport, he will probably find he can readily obtain some roughshooting and excellent pigeon shooting with bed and board in farm houses in various parts of the countryside on very reasonable terms. Once he has gained experience in this way he will be in a far better position to obtain pigeon shooting in the locality of his choice.

For the person who lives on the outskirts of a city or town, or in the country, the problem is usually much easier to solve, although either of the solutions so far offered may be suitable. Alternatively, in these circumstances, it is generally simple enough to find a large estate within reasonable distance where the services of a regular beater at the shoots will be welcome. By beating regularly, which can in itself be an enjoyable experience, he will find himself in the company of people who know where pigeon shooting is likely to be available. There are likely to be farm workers, or others, who may be keen pigeon shots themselves, or who may know where pigeon shooting is available for the asking. There will be gamekeepers, who in return for help in building release pens, or similar tasks, may offer both pigeon and rabbit shooting outside the shooting season.

Once the individual has gained the confidence of his fellow beaters and of the gamekeepers by showing his enthusiasm and readiness to learn it is likely that many doors will open to him. In order to gain access to a country sport such as pigeon shooting it is a sound policy to show enthusiasm for ancillary pursuits such as beating, trapping, ferreting and dog work. In the process a lot of value may be learned as well as a good deal of enjoyment obtained.

In whatever way the prospective pigeon shooter finally secures his shooting, whether through a club, in partnership with others, or by himself, he is unlikely in his first season to have opportunities for more than shooting over decoys, or flighting in to roost from ground level, unless he is very fortunate. Of course, much must depend on the part of the country in which he lives. In the south, with a few exceptions, platforms are not very common, but if he lives in the Midlands or further north, they are by no means unusual.

Unless he lives in an area where platform shooting is commonplace he may again find that his best solution is to check the advertisements, or consult with knowledgeable friends and, if necessary, continue making enquiries until he finds someone prepared to offer this form of shooting. There are certainly areas where such shooting may be obtained comparatively easily. In general, shooting from treetop platforms at pigeons may be found on estates where high seats built for roe shooting are also used at other times of the year for flighting pigeons in to roost. In most cases these platforms have been built primarily for roe shooting, or else deliberately as dual-purpose platforms, but there are increasingly places where they have been built specifically for pigeon shooting. This is generally the case where they are mounted in the trees themselves, or where platforms made from tubular steel have been erected for the purpose. Once the pigeon shooter has gained experience it may be that he will be able to introduce this form of shooting on his own home ground.

Wherever there are hills and valleys with some afforestation, platform hides may be used effectively and easily to provide sporting pigeon shooting from treetop level, or from above. Shooting feral birds in quarries may also be available providing sport on several levels. However, it is unlikely that in his first season the novice pigeon shooter will gain any experience of clifftop shooting at feral birds, though this can undoubtedly provide shooting of considerable interest. Since it is not a sport which is known or recognised by many except those who live near suitable terrain, it is generally necessary to study a map and make local enquiries.

Careful mapreading can save considerable time prior to prospecting suitable sites for clifftop or quarry shooting.

There are a surprisingly large number of suitable places which are simply ignored because people have not thought of them in these terms. Few people are fortunate enough, however, to have them on their doorstep and it may require time and perseverance to find suitable ground. As has been pointed out already, however, the same problem applies to finding any form of shooting. The city-bound pigeon shooting aspirant is thus really in a very difficult situation during his first year or so, for until he gains experience he is in no position to judge what is required. To a large extent he will have to rely on the advice of others until he can begin to trust his own judgment.

The gun and cartridges

The choice of a gun for pigeon shooting, or indeed in any shooting, must rest entirely with the individual concerned, but beware of too much involvement with guns, for this can lead on to gun collecting and can easily become an obsession. In any form of shooting it is the man behind the gun that counts, for it is not the gun that misses. Excepting only faulty cartridges, if the gun is fired at a pigeon within reasonable range at the right time in the right manner the bird will fall dead. Almost all misses are due to gun thrombosis, the clot behind the gun.

The problem of what sort of gun to use for pigeon shooting still remains a real one if the prospective pigeon shooter does not possess one. Whether he buys an over-and-under, or a side-by-side, must be a matter for personal preference. The former provides a single shooting plane, which some people prefer, while there are those who find the latter easier to load, especially inside the often limited confines of a hide. If finances are a problem a single barrel may suffice, but fewer birds will be shot. The best possible thing that anyone can do in this position is to place himself in the hands of his nearest reputable gunsmith, who will undoubtedly do his best to provide him with a suitable gun, always provided that he is over seventeen and has a shotgun certificate issued by the police.

Any good gunsmith will wish to provide a customer with sound professional advice, since satisfied customers are likely to return, and gunsmiths depend on customer goodwill to remain solvent. It is sensible therefore to explain the type of shooting for which the gun is required and to indicate clear price limits. Then make your personal choice within those limits. Once a choice has been made it is worth the small extra expense of having the gun properly fitted and tried out at the shooting school, if only to provide confidence, which is half the battle in any form of shooting.

Within reasonable price limits today the best bargains are probably some of the Spanish, Italian or Russian guns available, whether side-by-side, or over-and-under. The English side-by-sides are sadly now almost priced out of the market and old guns tend to have an antique value far beyond any relation to their use as a shotgun. First-class guns are best regarded simply as investments, or reserved for perfect driven days, rather than risking damage to them by shooting pigeons from a dirty ditch, or swaying treetop platform.

There are, of course, those who will advise buying a single barrel pump gun, or automatic, as the only suitable gun for pigeon shooting. Like any other type of gun, either of these can be perfectly satisfactory in the right hands and when birds are coming one after another in three's and four's they can sometimes prove very useful. It must be appreciated, however, that in the hands of inexperienced or reckless shots they are open to abuse. With such guns, even more than others, it is important to take well placed shots and kill each bird. The unfortunate fact is that with these guns it is possible to fire three, or even five, shots in quick succession, but sadly this does not mean that three, or five, birds are dead. Such a fusillade is much more likely to result in just one or two birds pricked or badly wounded, only to die later, lost to the bag.

It requires considerable practice and self-control to use either of these types of gun with any real degree of success.

One valid argument against them is that their balance tends to vary with each shot fired, which makes accurate shooting difficult. Another is that the average person simply does not have time to fire more than two properly aimed shots at a bird while it remains in range. This is especially true when shooting at pigeons. To fire off as many as five cartridges at one bird is not only unsporting and utterly deplorable, but also quite pointless and a waste of expensive ammunition. Both these types of gun also suffer from the major disadvantage that it is not possible to tell by merely looking at them whether they are loaded or not. It is also now illegal to use an automatic with more than three cartridges, except against pests, including pigeons, causing serious damage to crops. It is, however, up to everyone to decide for himself what suits him best.

There are, for instance, those who inveigh against the .410 shotgun. Yet for pigeon decoying there are occasions when a .410 can have distinct advantages, not least because the sound of the shot carries far less than that of a twelve-bore. With a long 3-inch cartridge the .410 can kill effectively at up to twenty-five yards and that may well be the distance at which most of the pigeons are coming in to the decoys. The counter argument, of course, is that not all birds are likely to come in so close and that beyond that range the .410 is more likely to wound than kill cleanly. One solution might be to use a .410 adaptor which simply slips inside the breech of a twelve-bore gun and enables a .410 cartridge to be fired. Both a .410 and/or one or more adaptors are worth including in the pigeon shooter's armoury if possible.

Whatever gun is used it is essential to know its limitations and best killing ranges. Quite a few birds throughout the year, including pigeons, are missed by taking shots too close, or too hurriedly, even if more are missed by shooting at too great a range. The latter, however, is generally the worse fault since so frequently in these circumstance a bird is pricked with one or two pellets causing it to die later only to provide fodder for foxes or carrion crows. The sight, however, of feathers flying from a wood-pigeon after a shot has been fired does not necessarily mean it has been hit. A pellet close to its body will often dislodge an astonishingly large number of feathers, yet it will continue unharmed.

This is not always the case, however, and it is thus extremely important to learn to visualise ranges so that shots are neither taken too close, nor at too great a distance. It is a good plan to get into the habit of estimating range by using a length which is easily visualised mentally, such as a cricket pitch, twenty-two yards long. Thus an object mentally estimated as being two cricket pitches away should be about forty yards, or the full range of a normal shotgun. As an aid to estimating height it is worth remembering that few trees are more than sixty feet high, therefore a bird flying over treetops is probably not more than twenty to thirty yards above ground. It is important to practice estimating ranges, checking them at first, if necessary, by pacing them out, until it becomes second nature to know whether a bird is within range.

When a gunsmith fits and tries a gun for a customer he will usually pattern it at forty yards. The pattern is merely the spread of shot, which is generally checked by firing at a steel plate newly covered with whitewash and then seeing how many pellets are within a thirty inch circle at that distance. The pattern should be judged for its uniformity and even density, without gaps through which a bird might fly. The number of pellets within the thirty inch circle should be counted each time and a series of shots, using cartridges with different charges of powder and loads and sizes of shot, should be fired to find those best suited to the gun. In general the shot sizes usually producing the best patterns for most guns are No. 6 and No. 7, if only because there are more pellets in each cartridge than with larger shot.

It is surely by now a long exploded fallacy that pigeons require heavy shot, or heavy loads, to bring them down. To use alphamax, or heavy shot, as if for wildfowl, when pigeon shooting is an absurdity. It leads, inevitably, to taking shots far out of range and to wounding birds that are never recovered and are left instead to die a miserable lingering death. This sort of behaviour is generally seen in the individual who has once had a lucky shot with some such cartridge and killed a bird that would normally be far out of range. Ever since that event he has been attempting to emulate the performance, failing to appreciate that in fact he is handicapping himself. It is only necessary to plate such cartridges at forty yards and then compare the pattern with that of ordinary load of No. 6 or 7 shot to see which is preferable for normal shooting.

Incidentally if no steel plate is available against which to check the pattern on a whitewashed background, a plastic sack, slit in half with a knife and hung over a fence or wall, at forty yards, provides a good substitute method of checking the pattern effectively. At a pinch a copy of *The Times* has also been known to serve the purpose. If only to gain confidence in one's cartridges, plating the gun occasionally is a useful exercise.

It is when plating a gun in this manner that the full effects of choke on the pattern will be seen and properly understood. The choke is merely the constriction at the end of the barrel, the degree of which determines the spread of the shot pattern. The degree of choke varies from True Cylinder, which as the name implies is none at all, through Improved Cylinder, the smallest degree of choke, to Quarter Choke, Half Choke, Three-quarter Choke and finally Full Choke. The names more or less speak for themselves.

Full choke will deliver the entire load of a normal No.6 cartridge within the thirty inch circle at forty yards. If hit at closer ranges the birds will tend to be very full of shot and almost uneatable, hence the commonest arrangement for normal all-round shooting is to have the right barrel Improved Cylinder and the left either Half, or Three-quarter Choke. This is as good as any for pigeon shooting. If taken within forty yards in the full pattern of an ordinary twelve-bore, Improved Cylinder, with a standard load of No. 6 or 7 shot, a pigeon will fall stone dead.

It may be permissible, even desirable, when shooting wood-pigeons flighting, or feral birds on the cliffs, to use a slightly heavier load if it suits the gun. This is really only to give the shooter more confidence in his ability to hit those high, fast birds, but confidence is all-important. In practice, if the gun is pointed in the right direction and swung freely even a light load will probably be just as successful.

Everyone will always shoot better in whatever circumstances if using cartridges in which they have confidence and to which they are accustomed. Otherwise there is bound to be a little nagging doubt at the back of the mind. After one or two unexpected misses a natural loss of confidence can lead to faults such as poking, or hesitating. This in turn can lead to more birds missed, or worse still wounded, and a spoiled day. Such things can happen to anyone for the most trivial reasons and are best avoided whenever possible. All shooting depends ultimately on confidence and concentration and loss of either can result in the best of shots performing abysmally.

It may be that the pigeon shooter prefers to load his own cartridges. Home-loading, like gun collecting, can very easily become something of an obsession, for each home-loader in the end begins to feel he can produce the perfect cartridge. It can indeed become almost a vice. Having said that, there is undoubtedly a certain pleasure in firing one's own cartridges and it is, in the end, undoubtedly cheaper. Against that has to be weighed the considerable initial expense of equipment, the necessity of setting aside the requisite space to commence operations and store the powder, shot, caps, empty cases and loading gear where it will be safe, as well as the considerable time and trouble involved. There are almost certainly more home-loaders who have given it up because they could not spare the time, or because of safety factors, than there are those who continue to produce their own cartridges, but there will always be some who prefer to do so.

Whatever cartridges are used it is always desirable to have something to hold them, rather than trying to carry some in an inaccessible cartridge belt and the remainder weighing down various pockets. If the pigeon shooter is also a game shot he will probably have a cartridge bag already. In practice any stout canvas bag, such as can be obtained in any surplus stores, will be perfectly adequate. It is, however, useful to have a bag which will hold 200 to 250 cartridges and which is fitted with a shoulder strap. If any more cartridges are likely to be needed these can be carried in their packs of twenty-five in some other container, such as a game bag.

To sum up then, the choice of a gun and cartridges must depend on the individual, but the choice of the gun once made, the choice of the cartridges must follow accordingly to suit the gun. It may be that finance dictates the choice, or it may be that physical or similar considerations are involved, such as the need for a light twenty-bore to compensate for a weak arm, or a crossover stock for a sight defect. In any event, as well as a heavier bore gun, a .410, or at the least a .410 adaptor, or pair of adaptors, should be included in the armoury if possible.

It is also desirable to have an air rifle available on occasions. In ruined buildings, or in farm buildings where a twelve-bore, or even a .410, might be dangerous, liable to cause damage or alarm stock, an air rifle can sometimes be used with great effect. Picking off pigeons that have alighted on roofs, cornices, gutters, or similar places, can prove a test of marksmanship and provide good sport as well as sometimes surprisingly large bags.

Finally it should be added that guns are valuable pieces of equipment and it pays to look after them, both in use and transit. In journeying to and from the shoot your car may have to traverse some rough ground, resulting in its contents being heavily jolted or thrown about. If you have a solid leather guncase with brass, or leather, reinforced corners in which the gun can be kept when travelling, so much the better, for its barrels are in less danger of being dented. It may take up a little room, but it will protect the gun and hold the essential cleaning materials.

A well-padded gunsleeve which zips all the way round so that it can be easily dried out when necessary, and fitted with a shoulder strap, is useful for carrying the gun from the car to the hide, or platform. It is possible to obtain these gunsleeves in canvas, P.V.C. or in leather with a kapok or sheepskin lining. If it can be afforded, the latter is preferable, as the combination of leather and sheepskin provides extra protection against accidental knocks. However, if the pigeon shooter is also a game shot he probably owns one anyway. If he does not, he should invest in one for it will prove its worth time and again.

If it has been raining during the day and the gun is wet, or muddy, it is important to dry it off thoroughly before starting to clean it. The use of a pipe-cleaner to dry out the difficult corners between the ribs and barrels is a useful tip. If the gun is put into a baize-lined guncase in a soaking wet state, rust will soon result. The guncase too must be thoroughly dried before being used again.

When the gun has been taken apart and dried and cleaned, a thin coating of oil should be applied internally and externally to the barrels and to the action. Be careful, however, not to get gun oil onto the stock, for this can have the effect of rotting the wood round the action. The stock is best treated separately with linseed oil. Do not forget, however, to pull the gun through before next shooting, to remove the oil which may otherwise affect the pattern of the first shots fired. Always treat your gun with care.

Gun safety

It is really not advisable to use a .22 rifle on pigeons, since there are only very rare occasions when it might be safe or even desirable to do so. The .22 is a highly lethal weapon with a possible range of over a mile and although there may be a few occasions when it could be used safely over decoys, where there is a safe background, the fact remains that even then a ricochet might travel a great deal further than intended, causing serious injury, if not death, to some innocent passer-by or animal. Yet dangerous though a .22 rifle may be, it should always be remembered that a shotgun in most cases is far more dangerous. The effect of a shotgun blast on flesh and bone at close range is horrific and totally irreparable. In a limb it may mean amputation; in the body, death.

The importance of gun safety cannot be over-stressed. It is essential at all times to conduct oneself as if the gun being handled is loaded, **even when it is known to be empty**. It is easy when shooting by oneself to get into very idle habits, but there is absolutely no excuse for it. In fact it is even more important to have a care when alone, for it is in moments of absent-mindedness that accidents so easily happen when aid is not readily at hand.

Do not forget to unload whenever leaving a hide, even if only going out for a moment or two to put out more decoys. Make sure the gun is unloaded.

No gun is safe unless it is empty and seen to be empty.

It is, of course, important never to site a hide anywhere near a public road or footpath where people might be walking. Similarly, any shots near grazing cattle or livestock of any kind should be avoided. Largely from the point of view of personal safety, as a matter of course, when siting decoys or taking a stand to flight pigeons, make absolutely certain there are no overhead cables or fence wires within range which could cause pellets to ricochet to your own or anyone else's danger. A ricocheting pellet may cost the sight of an eye in these circumstances.

All shotguns are potentially lethal weapons so always make sure your gun is unloaded when not in use. If necessary re-check and get into the habit of always checking. No-one will think any the less of a man who is doubly careful.

The best advice is easily summarised:

Treat all guns as loaded even when known to be unloaded.

4

Equipment on Various Levels

In pigeon shooting, as in any other form of shooting, it is
desirable to have all the necessary equipment to hand to
ensure a good day's sport, while at the same time avoiding
the mistake of overdoing it. It is easy enough to become
so keen on minor aspects of one's sport that the main object
is forgotten. There is the man who is so keen on guns he
has dozens of them and can never decide which one to use.
The truth is he really prefers collecting guns to shooting.
Home cartridge making, decoy production, or hide building
can all become art forms in their own rights if they are
allowed to do so and seriously distract attention from the
business of shooting pigeons. As far as equipment goes it
is desirable to keep it as simple as possible. Even then it
has a habit of accumulating in alarming quantities.

As already noted, the gun and cartridges are the first
and most important items required. At a pinch almost
everything else could be dispensed with and pigeons could
still be shot successfully without them, but there are some
items which undoubtedly can be helpful.

Maps

While not generally required while pigeon shooting, maps
of the ground are an essential pre-requisite and one which
is often overlooked. In the first place, as with any shooting,
they are a considerable aid to establishing the boundaries.
Then, apart from their considerable value in prospecting
for clifftop shooting and finding quarries which might
provide sport, the Ordnance Survey maps are vital when

Spying out the ground at the start of the day, when the binoculars are an essential item of equipment.

it comes to shooting pigeons in any area. By examining them closely and studying the lie of the land it is possible to work out the various likely pigeon movements, taking into account the various woodlands and contours. Having worked out likely bird movements, it is necessary to follow this through with observation on the ground. By filling in the various field crops and feeding available for the pigeons over a three- or four-thousand acre area it should be perfectly feasible to work out their likely feeding grounds and plan ahead accordingly.

Binoculars

The first major adjunct which only the pigeon shooter, as opposed to game shooter, requires, is a useful pair of binoculars. A monocular will do, if you prefer it, but nowadays useful pairs of binoculars can be bought so cheaply it is well worth investing in a good pair, with or without a zoom lens, which will make the business of checking on the movements of distant birds a pleasure rather than a problem.

For any serious pigeon shooting, this is by far the most important piece of equipment next to shotgun and cartridges. Even the fortunate individual with hawkeye vision will frequently find it hard to tell the difference between a flock of feeding pigeons and golden plover at a distance of half a mile. Using a good pair of glasses it is possible to check from a car with very little trouble the lines on which pigeons are moving and where they are feeding. The battle is then half won before it has started.

Decoys and supports

Another item of equal importance which the pigeon shooter requires is decoys and this is such an important matter that it merits a chapter to itself. (See Chap. 7) All that needs to be pointed out here is that this is yet another piece of equipment which has to be carried to the hide. Already the pigeon shooter has a gun and cartridges, plus binoculars. Now he has to add to that at least half a dozen decoys and this is only the beginning.

Depending on the types of decoys used it may be necessary to provide supports for them. If dead birds are being used, all that is really required in practice is a number of tealers, or short lengths of wood with a sharpened point, or similar lengths of reasonably stiff wire, to support the head of each in a lifelike way. Wire coathangers can be very easily twisted into useful supports when using dead birds as decoys, but they are liable to become just another piece of clutter to carry around. Extra tealers can usually be cut from a hedge, but there are those who advocate carrying a roll of wire which can be cut into suitable lengths to support decoy birds realistically.

Billhook or secateurs

Another item of nearly equal importance, which almost always proves useful is a really well sharpened billhook. It is not easy to obtain one nowadays, but it remains one of the best slashing and cutting tools to be found. It will cut almost anything from small saplings to brambles, nettles, or any form of greenery. For producing the materials for a hide in the shortest space of time a billhook is almost unbeatable. It does not take up much room and yet for hide building it is first-class. Folding billhooks, though not quite so good, are easier to carry and probably easier to obtain. Failing a billhook, a pair of strong secateurs may be used to cut most of the brambles, greenery and similar material used for the hide.

In general, wherever there is suitable cover, there is no need for any other aids to building a hide, and hide building is another matter of such importance that it merits a chapter to itself. (See Chap. 6) As will have been gathered, the billhook features prominently in this chapter.

Nets and supports

Two other items of equipment connected with hide building which may be required from time to time and which are certainly useful had also better be mentioned here, even if they may not always be wanted. The first of these is one, or better still two, of the modern camouflage nets which fold up so neatly that they can be fitted easiily enough into a hare pocket. The other is two or three pointed metal supports which can be stuck firmly into the ground and on which the netting may be hung to provide cover for the pigeon shooter. These should be about 4ft 6 in. long, made with a projection some 18 in. from the foot so that they can be dug into hard ground, with another about half-way, and a bifurcated top so that the netting can be strung over them.

Birdscarers

An occasional item of equipment which can be useful and is not often mentioned is a set of squib-type bangers. These can be set alight and guaranteed to burn off slowly, providing a loud bang every twenty minutes to half-an-hour for as long as is required. If there are signs that pigeons are feeding close-by, or that there is some alternative attraction, this can be a useful way of deterring them and driving them over towards the decoys that have been set out for them. The echo of a shot can sometimes have a very similar effect and it is always worth noting wherever the terrain provides an echo with a view to using it in this way if possible.

A light-weight ladder

This is a piece of equipment which some years ago I would never have regarded as of any importance, but since having acquired it I have found increasingly useful. Mine is a light 30 ft aluminium extending ladder. When it comes to investigating suitable platform hides in trees it is of the first importance. It can also be extremely helpful when it comes to lofting decoys in tricky places. Not only that, however, but it has been forcibly brought to my attention that, even in estates which are well keepered, leaving ladders, permanently attached to hides is not always safe. They have a more or less countrywide habit of disappearing. This is where the light aluminium extending ladder again comes into its own. If there are several platform hides in any area, it is simply a question of taking the ladder round and setting each gun in turn in position. When the time comes to finish for the day, it is taken round again and down they come in turn. In the intervals between shoots no evil minded individual can steal the ladder, because there is none to be stolen. Nor can any unauthorised person enter the hide and shoot pigeons from it.

Using an aluminum extending ladder to loft a decoy in the treetops.

Tide tables

An up-to-date set of tide tables is an item of equipment which can be absolutely vital when it comes to clifftop shooting for feral birds. These give the times of the tides around the coasts of Britain and from them it is easy to calculate when the tides will be in or out in any desired area. For the man below this can often be a matter literally of life and death, and one of the most important aspects of prospecting any clifftop shooting is to work out how long it takes to walk any given length of cliff so that the man below is not caught by the tide.

Retrieving birds from an ebb tide at the foot of the cliffs. It is essential to consult the tide tables and allow plenty of time.

Two-way radio

Whenever one or more guns are out together there is no doubt that being able to converse with one another easily and quietly over a distance can be very useful. A two-way radio can be a boon at times. When, for instance, the pigeon shooter wishes to inform his partner that birds are flighting in to a neighbouring field, or when the man at the foot of the cliff wishes to warn his companion that there is a nasty overhang not visible to him from above which is new since they last traversed that particular stretch, or when the man above wishes to tell his partner below that there are two birds to pick further forward, and so on, then it really proves its worth.

Although the walkie-talkie is a fairly modern adjunct to shooting it is still not as widely used as might be expected. For easy communication between the partners in clifftop shooting especially it makes life a lot simpler. It can also prove very helpful when it comes to flighting birds in to roost. If two or three guns are spread around a wood, occasional comments as to how birds are coming may make a great deal of difference. Whereas one previously relied on hearing shots fired and possibly missed the fact that birds were coming into an unguarded section, it is now possible to cover very much larger areas effectively and get the best sport available.

The dog

Although some pigeon shooters may disagree, I have always felt that one other requirement, without which no shooting would be worthwhile at least to me, must be a dog. It does not matter what sort of breed is preferred; it seems to me that in any form of shooting the company of a dog provides something important which is otherwise missing. Admittedly when shooting over decoys the dog must be trained to mark birds which fall far out, it must also learn not to touch the decoys, and it should be a fast and accurate retriever. From a platform hide, or flight shooting, the dog must be an independent and single-minded worker able to mark a bird by ear when it hears it fall and fetch it to the foot of the tree where its master is stationed. With some experience this soon becomes second nature.

When walking up woodland rides, or in clifftop shooting, a dog comes into its own. Then a retriever is extremely useful. Once it has learned what clifftop shooting involves it will not attempt to go over the edge, although there may be some heart-stopping moments in the early days. Down below, however, amongst the seaweed and wrack of the tideline, sometimes swimming out to sea for occasional retrieves, or plunging into rock pools, the dog will have ample work to keep him busy.

Only if shooting from a boat is a dog definitely not desirable. Unless the sea is remarkably calm it is unlikely in my experience that there will be many birds to pick, but for those few a long-handled fishing net is the best answer. A wet dog shaking itself all over everyone in the confined space of a small boat is nobody's idea of amusement and is unlikely to add to the owner's popularity. It is much better avoided by leaving the dog behind on such occasions.

Personal comfort, camouflage and equipment

When it comes to shooting from a hide it is desirable to have some sort of face covering. Face masks can be bought, but seem really a somewhat unnecessary expense. Either a perfectly ordinary balaclava in some sort of khaki or similar material can be worn, although in warm weather this can become unbearably hot and itchy, or else a stocking mask can be very easily made from a pair of nylon tights of suitable greenish colouring. This too can become extremely warm. A handful of mud, or earth, smeared on the hands and then on the face is probably as good as anything, being very easily washed off at the end of the day and fully as effective as anything else.

From the clothing viewpoint any suitable clothing merging with the background will do. Government surplus camouflage clothing is readily available and a hat and jacket are well worth buying. If you also invest in a pair of trousers, you need little more to merge with the landscape. In a hide, with the hands covered by mitts or mud, the head by a hat, and the face by a covering of either mud or cloth, a suitable merging jacket is all that is really required.

Another essential item of equipment for ordinary decoy shooting from a hide is something on which to sit comfortably. This has to provide a conveniently broad base, which can if necessary be padded with a folded sack. A five-gallon oil drum used to be a favourite answer at one time, being readily available on most farms, easily enough transported and quite comfortable. Nowadays a five-gallon plastic bucket, which can be bought very cheaply, is an even better answer since it can be used to carry a sack, spare cartridges and similar items, including beer and sandwiches to the hide, and after a good day it can always be used for carrying those extra birds which would not fit into the sack. The adjustable type of shooting stick, which has a wing nut to adjust the shaft to half-length is heavy to carry and no more comfortable or convenient.

A game bag is yet another item of equipment the average game shooter will possess, which can be very useful for pigeon shooting. It can be used to carry extra cartridges, decoys, and a folded sack when going to the hide and on the way back can be used to carry those birds which cannot be accommodated in the sack. To either game- or cartridge-bag it is worth attaching a cartridge extractor by a piece of stout cord. It may never be used, but equally a day can easily be spoiled when a cartridge has jammed irretrievably and this vital piece of equipment is not available.

Two other items, which should always be at least available in the car to slip in a pocket when they might be required, are a torch and an insect repellent spray. By this time, however, the prospective pigeon shooter will be carrying a gun in a gunsleeve over one shoulder, cartridges in a cartridge bag over another, binoculars in a case in one pocket, a camouflage net in another, more cartridges if necessary, plus a folded sack and a billhook in a gamebag on his back, with a five-gallon bucket containing beer and sandwiches and decoys in one hand and metal supports for the hide in the other. He will not wish to carry much more for any distance.

There is one final piece of equipment which is all too often overlooked by the novice and that is a game larder. In hot weather especially the danger of pigeons becoming fly-blown is very real. After a good day's shooting in warm Spring weather, or in mid-Summer, any shot birds can become fly-blown very quickly indeed. It is hopeless to expect to keep any birds from becoming thoroughly fly-blown and totally unfit for eating unless they are kept in a suitably fly-proof game larder.

Game larders large enough to hold two or three hundred pigeons, with sufficient space to allow air to circulate freely around them as well as keeping them fly-proof, tend to be expensive. A good cheap and efficient substitute can be readily produced by buying a suitable stoutly-built old wardrobe in the salerooms, where one can usually be bought very cheaply indeed. The first necessity is to remove any shelving inside so that the interior is bare. Then remove the panels of the door and sides. Replace them with nylon net curtain material glued to the framework, and an excellent entrance flap can be made very easily with velcro material. The result is an instantaneous and fully effective fly-proof game larder. With poles crossing the interior in place of the shelving there should be ample room for several hundred pigeons to hang in pairs so that air circulates around them freely.

5

Preparations on Various Levels

When permission has been obtained to shoot pigeons over a farm, or shooting has been rented or otherwise acquired, the first important move is to get to know the lie of the land as soon as possible. It is pointless hoping to shoot pigeons successfully unless the ground has been thoroughly covered on foot beforehand to get to know not only the farm itself, but the neighbouring area as well. Initially this may mean tramping round the fields and woods, using map and binoculars to prospect the ground, to try to work out the likely movements of pigeons over it and over the surrounding land. It will also mean touring the area in a car on by-roads and farm tracks to get to know it as thoroughly as possible, so that each landmark on the map is clear in the mind.

As has been pointed out, the Ordnance Survey map can be extremely useful to a pigeon shooter in more ways than one. For finding conveniently-placed quarries, or clifftop shooting, it is essential, unless such places are already known. For checking a large area of ground and working out where pigeons are likely to be feeding or roosting, it is invaluable. By marking on a tracing or photocopy the location of the various crops on the ground it is usually possible, even after the first visit, to make some intelligent advance assessments of the likely places where and periods when pigeons will be feeding. It is usually also possible to work out fairly quickly where the most likely roosting woods are to be found and mark them as well as the lines of passage observed, or those which it seems most likely pigeons will follow. It is then worth making preparations accordingly, by building semi-permanent hides in suitable well sited positions. In such circumstances there is always considerable satisfaction to be had when a good day results from preparations made far in advance.

Whatever the size of the area over which shooting has been obtained it is almost certain that it will be necessary to check the land around the boundaries, to work out where there are roosting woods, or crops, likely to be attractive to pigeons at various times of the year. It is pointless to consider an area of say 500 acres, or even 2000 acres, in total isolation from its surroundings. A large wood or series of woods, or fields of attractive feeding right on the boundaries or close to them, are bound to affect the movement of birds over quite a considerable area, even amounting to several square miles at times.

There are also bound to be occasions when prevailing weather conditions, a concentration of available feeding, or similar circumstances, draw birds into one particular feeding or roosting ground, quite possibly outside the boundaries of the shooting available. For instance it may be that there is only one field of kale showing above the surface after a brief snowfall, or one cornfield in an area badly laid, into which literally hundreds of birds are flocking. It is frequently possible to foresee such events and prepare for them by siting hides where birds may be intercepted in passage to and from the ground in question. In the cases quoted, for instance, the sheltered position of the one field and the exposed position of the other might have been noted beforehand. Such events can only be foreseen, however, by studying all the ground in the immediate neighbourhood for quite a way around.

It is advisable always to know as far as possible what is being grown on the neighbouring ground, so that when a pigeon is shot an examination of the crop contents can provide a fairly accurate answer as to where it has been feeding. By taking a car and the binoculars on a circular tour on the morning of the day intended for shooting it is usually possible to establish the flight lines to the feeding grounds fairly quickly. In any area which has been thoroughly checked both on the map and on the ground itself, it should not take long to decide where the bulk of the pigeons are feeding. The correctness, or otherwise, of this assessment will be quickly established after one or two have been shot on the flight lines to the feeding grounds and their crops have been examined. The pigeon shooter can then take action accordingly.

Inspection of the crops of all pigeons shot can very often provide some useful pointers for future shooting. At the end of any day it is always an important part of the proceedings to empty their crops. In the first place this prepares them for hanging and secondly provides a considerable insight into their feeding habits. It will usually indicate reasonably clearly to anyone with a sound knowledge of the ground where they have been feeding most recently. It is also an opportunity to rid the crops of any fresh green feed, which is otherwise likely to contaminate the flesh of the bird. Around harvest time, as indicated earlier, it may also provide enough grain to feed a number of hens, or alternatively supply some extra feed for any game that is being reared or conserved.

Just as it is always important to bear in mind what the pigeons' favourite feeding is likely to be at any given time, so it is a good plan to think ahead to the month to come. It should be possible for an experienced pigeon shooter to review the ground mentally and decide where they are most likely to find that food. The next stage is to decide how to approach the ground with a view to shooting as many birds as possible. Assuming he knows the ground well and has prepared matters properly beforehand, it is probable that he has already placed some semi-permanent hides on the ground with a view to this situation arising. It is this ability to think like a wood-pigeon and look ahead to future possibilities which immediately gives the experienced pigeon shooter an advantage over his quarry.

By intelligent anticipation in this way, by using a map sensibly once the sowing plans for the coming year are known, the pigeon shooter can save himself a lot of trouble. It is not difficult to work out, for instance, that various fields of clover and early corn are likely to be prime targets in April and May, or that one or two fields of corn which are exposed to high winds may be laid and become targets for greedy pigeons on the laid crop in July and August and so on. Such really fairly elementary forecasting can save a lot of humping of hides and equipment later in the year.

It will, of course, also help enormously when it comes to making a reconnaissance if a shrewd idea has already been formed of what to expect and where to look. On the other hand it is equally essential to keep an open and flexible mind, to be ready to admit a mistake has been made and make a quick change of plan if the line of reasoning proves entirely wrong. There is nothing gained and quite a lot to be lost by stubbornly sticking to mistaken conclusions. If birds just are not where they were expected to be then the answer is look around until you find them and go there.

As an initial step it is desirable to know all the various crops growing on the farm and, if possible, learn to recognise them when they have been newly sown and are only just visible. This takes time and a lot of experience, but it will prove well worthwhile and most farmers will appreciate the effort involved. Furthermore, once birds have been shot as and when required and the results are seen, the efforts the shooting partnership, syndicate, or club, have made, will be thoroughly appreciated.

The following season it will be worth approaching neighbouring farms to enquire what their cropping plans are for the coming year. It should be explained that the reason for this enquiry is because you are shooting pigeons on the next door ground and their plans may affect the pigeons' movements. Such an approach, tactfully phrased, should be appreciated and might even result in an offer of more shooting. At the very least, the enquiry should receive a friendly reception and wholehearted co-operation.

Even on the rare occasions where this approach receives

a surly answer, it remains a sound policy to adopt and the general principle of trying to be a good neighbour is always advisable. It can do no harm and often does a lot of good. Simply making one's presence known in itself is useful so that when one is seen on the boundary or around the roads, a friendly wave is likely to replace a suspicious stare. By degrees the pigeon shooter and his partners, or companions, should become an accepted part of the local scene. This in turn may lead to friendly hints from tractor drivers, or other farm workers, as to the movement of birds, which at times can prove very useful. The offer of an occasional brace of birds will help to keep local relations on a friendly basis and taking the time for a friendly chat never does any harm as long as the day's work is not being interrupted. That will not go down at all well.

One other important preparation for the season's shooting is to check in advance all the suitable parking places for your car or van. It is as well to remember that what may seem a dry and suitable spot in summer may be a swampy quagmire in winter from which anything less than a land-rover will need to be ignominiously towed with many imprecations by an extremely disgruntled tractor driver. Even when the necessary equipment has been reduced to a minimum it is always useful to be able to drive your car, van, or land-rover as near as possible to the position finally chosen for the day's shooting. Having unloaded as close to the chosen site as feasible the vehicle should then be parked inconspicuously under cover and out of the way, even though the birds may be well used to the sight of it. The pigeon shooter may then get down to erecting the hide and setting out the decoys, having first ensured that any birds which were feeding have removed themselves out of sight.

Siting hides

Preparing hides in likely places long in advance of their use may, of course, be with a view either to shooting over decoys at feeding birds or for flighting birds in to roost. Wherever possible it is worth considering the possibility of building them with an eye to using them for both purposes. They should certainly not necessarily be restricted to one level only. It is often the case for example that a ditch provides a good natural hide below ground level for flighting birds at the edge of a wood, or for shooting over decoys. Equally it may be that a platform hide on the edge of a wood intended primarily for flighting can occasionally be usefully used for shooting over decoys placed in the field adjacent where pigeons are feeding.

Although more often than not hides used for shooting over decoys will be on ground level or below, there are exceptions. For instance, a stack of bales adjacent to a wood may provide a platform hide at treetop level for flighting birds in to roost, or it may make a perfectly good hide at treetop level for shooting over decoys on the ground. It always pays to look at pigeon shooting from all the various levels available, but as a first step it is essential to discuss the erection of any permanent or semi-permanent hides with the landowner beforehand and obtain his permission to build them. Clearly no hide should be allowed to interfere with drainage, or damage fences, growing trees, stacks of bales or in any way cause annoyance or loss to the landowner.

When it comes to making hides solely for shooting at birds coming in to roost in the evening, of course, platform hides can provide the greatest sport. This does not mean to say, however, that good sport cannot also be had with simple camouflage hides at the edge of the wood, or possibly without any hide at all in a suitable clearing in the centre of the wood where birds sometimes tend to drop in from a considerable height. A great deal must depend on the ground and the circumstances when it comes to flighting pigeons in to roost.

Once again, however, careful reconnaissance of the ground is always worthwhile. Where it is noted that a gun can be sited so that each shot provides an answering echo from, for instance, the side of a hill opposite, it is worth remembering that this method can sometimes be used effectively to drive birds towards rather than away from the gun. If this effect is observed it is well worth utilising it to the full. Where they can be used effectively such tactics can often mean a considerably increased bag.

Quarry shooting

When it comes to shooting in quarries an echo can also have a considerable effect, causing birds to move towards a waiting gun rather than away from him. An initial shot fired at the face of a quarry, or over the edge, will often result in the roosting birds flying wildly in all directions, some of them over the waiting gun. In general, however, it will be noticed that there are certain routes which they normally tend to follow.

The answer to shooting in or round any quarry is generally to take some time studying the movements of the birds. After their normal reactions have been checked it is worth experimenting by checking on their movements when disturbed from different angles. The direction of the prevailing wind will, as in most forms of pigeon shooting, have a considerable effect on their movements, but a pattern of some sort can usually be established. When such a pattern has emerged it is usually only a question of stationing two or three guns at suitable points to enjoy good sport. As with most forms of roost shooting, however, it is important not to overdo it and to stop while the birds are still coming in, otherwise they may desert the spot entirely and the pigeon shooter will have effectively ruined his own sport.

Cliff shooting

When it comes to shooting feral birds on the cliffs, however, there is generally little danger of overshooting the birds, regardless of how many cartridges may be fired. The

Shooting from a quarry edge at birds far below, where care and a head for heights are essential.

Shooting from a quarry edge at birds swirling over in the wind currents can provide very good sport.

important feature of cliff shooting is returning in one piece and it is by no means necessarily the man at the top of the cliff who is most at risk. Unless care is taken to consult the tide tables accurately and unless the ground has been thoroughly reconnoitred and the time normally taken to cover the ground has been carefully checked, it is quite easy in some places for the gun below to be caught by the tide and if he escapes with a wetting he has probably been lucky.

The reconnaissance of any pigeon shooting is important if you wish to shoot pigeons, but the reconnaissance of cliff shooting is important if you wish to survive. Having found a suitable coastline where there is a likely looking length of cliff which is reasonably approachable from underneath and from above the first thing is to check the tide tables and then walk it from below, checking how many colonies of feral birds are seen on the way. At the same time it should be noted where there are any noticeably dangerous looking overhangs, also points where it might be possible at a pinch to climb the face fairly easily in an emergency, such as being caught by advancing tides. Having thus prospected the possible shooting ground from below, for birds, as well as dangerous overhangs and possible escape routes, it is then time to check the route from above. Once satisfied that there is a possible stretch of clifftop shooting available, the next step is to approach the landowner and enquire whether he is willing to lease it. If he refuses, then of course, it is necessary to start prospecting elsewhere, but if he can be convinced of the prospective shooters' sincerity few landowners are likely to withhold some form of agreement and most farmers will be pleased to have the birds shot.

When making the initial reconnaissance, however, it is generally desirable for both partners involved to walk the bottom together first and then the top. If they are then able to rent the shooting they will each know both levels of the pigeon shooting and can take either with confidence. By using a walkie-talkie they should be able to converse

Caution and a head for heights are certainly pre-requisites for clifftop shooting.

comparatively easily, which is a considerable advantage. If a walkie-talkie is not available they will have to shout, or arrange a series of signals by whistle, or waving.

It is essential in cliff shooting for the partners to have some form of communication, even if it is only shouting. For the man above it is often decidedly dangerous to approach the edge too closely. On the other hand it is frequently hard to hear anything above the pounding of the waves and the shrieking of outraged gulls. A walkie-talkie makes life a great deal easier for both concerned, but even then it is not always easy as unless the aerials are visible to each other communication can be difficult. There is no doubt that in this form of shooting particularly it is advisable to check the ground and the weather carefully beforehand, but equally it has to be admitted that it provides sport which has a distinctly different flavour to it.

Woodland rides

The much more familiar inland version of the same sport is, of course, walking-up the rides of woods with two partners or more, driving the woodland rides to each other. Here again the first and most important element is to know the ground thoroughly. A large-scale map of the area is essential to obtain the best sport. From this it is usually possible to work out the best likely ways to approach the problem. Even so there is nothing to beat reconnaissance on the ground itself.

For a start, as no two stretches of cliff are the same, so no two woods are the same. Judging only from a map it might seem obviously desirable to approach a wood from one side, but on investigation on the ground it may well turn out that there are few if any birds on that side at all, while the other side is full of them. On the other hand, it may just be that the weather conditions are entirely wrong for a wood when it is first visited, but absolutely right on a second visit. There can be numerous reasons for having a good day and an equal number for a bad one. When things go well, however, this can provide as good sport as any and it has the virtue of having an extremely useful role for a dog, but as with any other form of pigeon shooting suitable preparation beforehand is essential to success.

Depending entirely on the size and shape of the wood the best plan may be for two guns to circle the wood, with one on the outside and one on an inner ride. Alternatively if the wood is split by regular drives into squares, as is usually the way with Forestry Commission woods, it may well be that a more effective method is for the guns to take parallel drives and walk one each side of each square, thus pushing the birds between them over the rides to provide each of them with shooting. In such circumstances they should normally arrange beforehand to halt when they reach each transverse crossing ride, at the end of each square of woodland, until they see that the other gun has also reached the end of the ride so that they know they are keeping level with each other the whole time. Otherwise while one may have been forced to halt when his dog was picking up a bird the other may have walked too far ahead, so that they have lost contact with each other and are no longer working in partnership.

The important point is that they must form a plan before they start and each must stick firmly to it. Once again a walkie-talkie set apiece can make a great deal of difference. Without a suitable means of communication, or a set plan of campaign, they can easily become separated in a large wood and totally fail to act effectively in concert. Given good preparation, sound co-operation and effective communication, however, they may both have good sport and quite often surprisingly good bags.

6

Hides on Various Levels

Before discussing the siting or building of hides it is as well to look at the purpose behind them and have that clear in the mind. Primitive man developed the use of camouflage to a high degree to disguise his presence from the game he was hunting. The use of plumed headdresses to break the stark outline of the head and of paint on the face to merge its colour with the background are merely two examples of methods used from man's earliest days. His ability to conceal himself behind bushes, trees, or vegetation were all part of primitive man's hunting skills developed over the centuries.

There are cave paintings extant in South Africa showing bushmen of the Kalahari holding a pole with an ostrich head on it, their bodies cloaked in feathers, stalking a herd of ostriches with bow and arrows. This is merely a primitive version of the stalking horse used by wildfowlers in the eighteenth century when a quiet old nag was utilised as cover for a wildfowler stalking geese. In the early years of this century a horse and cart were commonly used for stalking the Great Bustard in the plains of Hungary.

A stalking horse, whether real or contrived, was nothing more than a mobile hide intended to conceal the hunter until he was in a position to shoot his quarry. Since a hide is static its aim must be to conceal the person of the shooter in a convenient position to ambush his quarry. The siting of the hide is therefore all-important and the use of decoys placed to attract birds within range is really secondary, although in combination with the hide it can be of vital importance to the result.

All that is really required of any hide is to disguise the shape of the human form and avoid alarming the bird. As long as the bird, when looking in that direction, does not see the pigeon shooter and also sees nothing unusual to alarm it, the hide has fulfilled its purpose. Whether the bird sees an old tractor and trailer parked in a field corner, or a heap of potato boxes, an old hen house, or virtually any agricultural artifact to which it is accustomed, does not matter, as long as it does not see the pigeon shooter in the background. If on looking down the length of a hedge and ditch the wood-pigeon sees a slight bump in the ditch, but nothing seemingly to be alarmed about, then the pigeon shooter has camouflaged his position well. Although wood-pigeons are wary of unusual objects and quick to see the slightest movement within their somewhat limited range of vision, while in search of food they tend, like human beings, to see only what they expect to see.

When obtaining pigeon shooting one of the first considerations should be to obtain permission to build various permanent, or semi-permanent, hides. If an assurance is given that no damage will be caused and there will be no danger to stock involved there will usually be no objections raised. This will generally save a lot of time and trouble later on when time may be important. If early reconnaissance of the area has been carried out successfully it should be possible to work out reasonably accurately where the main roosting or assembly points for wood-pigeons are to be found, and from these the more commonly used flight-lines to the various feeding grounds. Much will inevitably depend on the direction and strength of the wind and also on weather conditions. Although wood-pigeons can be expected to conform to certain patterns of behaviour, differing winds and weather conditions will have a considerable effect on their movements, as with any animals or birds in the wild, but allowance should be made for this by siting alternative hides for different conditions.

The siting of permanent or semi-permanent hides also depends, like all hide building, on the materials available and the particular situation in question. They may, of course, be on several levels, from below ground to treetop level or above, depending on the ground and the purpose for which required, whether for flighting birds in to roost, for passage shooting, or for shooting over decoys. It is quite often a good plan, where suitable, to site two hides within range of each other, for use in different weather or wind conditions or, alternatively, for another gun to use at the same time. Siting two guns in one hide is not usually satisfactory since too often there is only shooting for one.

By using the map and advance knowledge of the crops it should be possible to make some reasonably intelligent forecasts as to useful places for hides even at the start of the first season's shooting. Once the commoner flight lines between likely assembly points and feeding places have been established it is always worth setting up a suitable semi-permanent hide on either side of any trees in a hedgerow en route which look as if they might attract wood-pigeons to perch. Hides sited within reasonable gunshot range of these can usually be expected to produce good results later in the year when conditions are suitable. The chances are that such trees frequently attract passing pigeons, but the use of a lofted decoy in such circumstances will very probably bring passing birds within range of a well placed hide. Another advantage of making permanent or semi-permanent hides, is that the wood-pigeons have time to get used to them and even if they happen to stand out a little the birds will become accustomed to them and eventually ignore them.

These permanent or semi-permanent hides may consist of little more than a screen of hedge deliberately encouraged to grow across a corner, or an elder or broom suitably pruned to provide both cover and a field of fire. A little work with a billhook may be all that is required. Alternatively a length of pig-netting or garden netting, good light stuff which can be readily curved into a suitable shape, leaving an entrance, can be set inside a fence and camouflaged with branches. These will require renewal at intervals, or natural growth may be encouraged up the sides of the netting. Simple constructions of this kind can be left in position around the shoot so that the birds become accustomed to them and they can be used when required.

It is desirable to see that such permanent or semi-permanent structures do not deteriorate into eyesores, but it is more important still to ensure that they are not in any way a danger to stock. It is in any event inadvisable to build such hides where stock might have access to them. They should always be securely behind wire and not only for the stock's sake, because there is nothing young bullocks like more than rubbing themselves against convenient posts. Even the stoutest of constructions is not likely to last very long in those circumstances.

Below-ground-level hides

Much must depend on the time of year and the place, as to the methods used to manufacture a hide. If a ditch is convenient it is often possible to use this effectively. A good, deep ditch, especially in summer, when it may be completely dry, can provide an excellent hide with little or no addition. It is quite often possible to set out the decoys and to take up a position in a ditch with some conveniently placed cover, such as an overhanging bush, and have a good day's sport. Perhaps because the pigeon-shooter's entire body is hidden from view below ground level a ditch hide can often prove surprisingly effective. In some cases it is worth constructing a platform to provide good footing, although at the same time making sure that this does not in any way affect the drainage. The possibility of a hide not in a ditch yet below ground level is not often considered, but it is sometimes well worthwhile digging a slit trench inside a fence on the edge of a wood, which may be used either for decoying, or flighting.

If permission has been obtained to dig a slit trench in a field this can sometimes prove a most effective hide, although often quite hard work. Just as useful at times

A decoy lofted on a fence post: the pigeon shooter in a drainage hole in front is almost invisible.

may be a similar hole dug by the farmer, or landowner, for drainage purposes, if it can conveniently be used. By seizing opportunist advantage of any such suitably placed hole and merely adding a length of camouflage netting, the pigeon shooter may save himself a lot of effort. Of course, whenever a hole is dug in a field to make a hide, it goes without saying that it must be filled in after the day's shooting is finished. To leave a hole in a field would be to invite the danger of stock being injured and having to be destroyed as a result. This is the sort of thoughtless behaviour which could well and rightly result in the shooting being lost.

Ground-level hides

During the summer months and into the autumn, bale hides can often prove useful, since the sight of bales around the countryside is unlikely to cause the pigeons any anxiety. There are, of course, two main types of bale to be seen, large and cylindrical, or small and oblong. Occasionally a third kind may be encountered which are small and cylindrical, but they may be dealt with in the same way as the small oblong bales.

The two methods of building a hide with these latter types of bales are fairly obvious and are largely a matter of common sense, each using up to sixteen or so bales. For one it is merely necessary to build three sides of an upright tower, four bales high on each side, with two or three bales providing cover on the top and perhaps one, or even two, bales in the open front, but allowing plenty of room for the gun to swing forward. A spare bale is best used as a seat. A gap can be left at one corner in front to allow for easy exit and entrance of the pigeon shooter and dog. It is always possible to leave gaps here and there in the framework to allow for all-round observation. The other type of bale-hide is four sided, having an open top and a gap at one corner for easy entrance and exit. It is largely a matter of personal preference which type is used.

Whenever building a bale hide it is very important to have well strung dry bales, if possible. There are few things worse than trying to handle wet bales with strings which come apart as they are grasped, leaving piles of soggy straw. In this, as in many other matters, the pigeon shooter is at the mercy of the farmer, however, and should be thankful for anything he cares to provide. On the other hand, the farmer in general should accept that it is in his own interests to help, if he wants the pigeons shot. When asked to provide bales the farmer will very probably drop them off in the field wherever it has been suggested is most suitable. The pigeon shooter should mark the spot clearly with some prominent marker such as a branch stuck firmly

Setting up a hide with metal supports and a billhook should only take a few minutes.

The hide only partially completed to show the pigeon shooter in position. Note face mask and glove. With a few minutes more work filling in back and sides as on the left of the picture he would be invisible.

in the ground, for if the bales are not where they are needed he may be in for some hard labour moving them across the field.

Bale hides are amongst the easiest and most useful to set up after harvest, since bales are then readily available on most farms. The best point about a bale hide is that it can be set up in the middle of a field in splendid isolation and can even be used with a lofted decoy set on the topmost bale to attract approaching birds to the decoys set out nearby. Although it may be desirable, it is certainly not true that such a hide has to be set up a day or several days beforehand to accustom the birds to its presence. As long as all the birds are driven off the field before the hide is built, there is no need to worry about pigeons not coming in to decoys set out nearby.

The difficulty with the large round bales, since they weigh about half a ton apiece, is that it normally requires a fork lift to move them. Depending on the lie of the ground it is sometimes possible to roll them a little way and, if there are two people working together, it is feasible to move them a certain amount, but even so they are extremely awkward to handle. They can, however, be used to make a good hide, either lying horizontally, or preferably standing on end, when two are put close together to leave a recess in which the pigeon shooter can sit. A length of nylon curtain material, dyed a near match to the straw, if pegged over the two bales with another length stretched in front, makes an effective hide. Oblong bales may be used instead of such material, if they are available.

Just as bales usually provide a good base for a hide, so do most hedges. With the use of a billhook a hide can usually be produced in most hedges fairly quickly without much difficulty. It is essential, however, that no damage is done to the hedge in the process. While a certain amount of trimming of an overgrown hedge may not come amiss, severe hacking about of a neatly trimmed hedge is not only bad practice, but is likely to cause ill-feeling. By the same token, chopping branches off growing trees, or causing damage to well grown trees, are other unnecessary ways of becoming unpopular. By all means cut elder, broom, gorse, or thorn, as long as the hedge is not damaged as a result, but keep within reasonable limits at all times and as a matter of sound practice do not leave newly severed branch ends showing as a warning signal. Elder and broom are usually the most convenient bushes for hide building, being easy to deal with and also providing the best cover.

This is where light metal steel supports for a hide can be invaluable. With three or four of these light metal rods it is possible to build a hide very quickly and effectively in almost any hedge within a few minutes. They can also be very useful in almost all forms of hide building and with the addition of a few yards of camouflage netting it is possible to build an extremely effective hide nearly anywhere with very little preparation. A roll of modern camouflage netting about 12 yards long by some 2 yards wide, which is about the minimum length required, can be carried quite easily in a poacher's pocket. Two such rolls are generally more than enough for most purposes.

Treetop-level hides

The building of hides below ground and at ground level is simple enough. When it comes to building hides at treetop level or above it becomes a little more complicated. The simplest raised hides that are readily available are probably the tops of hay or straw stacks. It is surprising how few people seem to think of using these as a useful base for a hide, yet quite often they are found alongside spinneys or young plantations where wood-pigeons are flighting in regularly. In such circumstances they can prove a very useful place for a hide. Furthermore it can sometimes prove suprisingly effective to shoot pigeons over decoys set out on the ground from the top of a stack rather than ground level.

It is sometimes possible to find a mound inside a wood which provides a near perfect position for shooting over the level of the trees, but most treetop level hides are platforms of one sort or another. As indicated earlier an aluminium ladder is invaluable to prospect positions for hides on this level. The hides themselves may be mounted on wooden supports, in the manner of wooden high seats built for roe shooting, for which they may well be used at times. Alternatively they may be made from tubular steel as in ordinary construction work and again may be used for roe as well. Such hides, whether of wood or metal, are usually four-sided towers of sturdy construction with wire guy ropes extending from each corner and secured to firmly bedded stakes or to nearby trees. Even so it will be found they will still rock in a high wind. The tubular steel towers can also be triangular, three-sided constructions, which in some ways are preferable as on the whole they are simpler to construct and even if they do not readily provide room for two, they are otherwise quite as effective as the more solid four-sided affairs.

The other type of treetop construction is the platform actually built into the tops of from one to four trees. The important thing here is to avoid damaging the trees by hammering nails into them, or breaking too many branches. On the whole, by using fencing wire nailed to wooden supports and encircling the tree trunks it is comparatively simple to build the base on which a platform can be laid. With pig netting, or similar fencing, up to above waist level, about 4 ft 6 in. high, nailed round the platform, suitably camouflaged with branches or by the growth of the tree or trees, the hide is complete. Knotted ropes, rope ladders, or ordinary ladders may all be used, but an aluminium extending ladder is almost certainly the most reliable means of access. Such a hide should provide several years of excellent sport before the growth of the tree or trees makes it necessary to move upwards, or elsewhere. Especially where sited in a young plantation, there usually comes a time when the trees in which the hide is sited grow so high it is necessary to raise the platform, or else the view is obscured by the growth of the surrounding trees.

Using a roe platform for flighting birds in to roost can provide good sport.

The higher the treetop hide, of course, the greater the amount of sway there is in any sort of wind. Even when a tower hide is well anchored by guy ropes or wires, it can be quite a seasick-making experience standing in them for any length of time. They are not nearly as bad, however, as the hides fixed to the treetops themselves. The amount of sway in some of these can be distinctly alarming and on occasions quite enough to excuse any number of misses. On the other hand the satisfaction from the birds killed in these circumstances is usually enough to make up for any such discomforts.

It is most important in any treetop-level hides to make sure they are safe. This is not just a question of providing a railing about 4 ft 6 in. up from the base. It is also important to make sure that the wooden base provides a sound grip for the feet. Since these bases are left out in all weathers they tend to become very slimy and greasy. The best answer is perhaps to nail thin treads underfoot, but even these can become slippery. Another solution is to make a tarred and gritted surface to provide a suitable grip for the feet. The snag to this must surely be that in very hot weather in mid-summer there must be an unpleasant tendency for the tar to melt. Wire netting nailed to the base can be effective, but on the whole a bucketful of sand or grit, applied immediately before shooting, is probably as good a solution as any.

Anyone with much experience of treetop hides will have found they vary from the palatial to the lunatic, and some cannot be classified as particularly safe. On occasions the yachting principle of using a safety line might be a good idea, with one end round the pigeon shooter's waist and the other end secured to the platform. The only snag with this, of course, is that if the entire platform takes off in the wind being secured to it might not be the best idea. This is not to say that, despite their occasional susceptibility to wind, treetop hides are not great fun. They undoubtedly are and shooting from them can provide enormous sport.

Treetop platforms may 'vary from the palatial to the lunatic'. An aluminum extending ladder would have been an asset here

If shooting at treetop level is always likely to be interesting and liable sometimes to cause vertigo, to shoot from above at high birds flighting over treetops some forty yards below also has a fascination all its own. Nevertheless anyone with any weakness for heights is advised to give it a miss. On the other hand, if the shooter is fit and unaffected by heights, this can provide some extraordinarily unusual shooting when a suitable site has been found for it. The first time I ever met this type of shooting was in the valley of the Findhorn. On a cliff point some 250 feet up I was placed above a well grown plantation and shot high pigeons flighting over the trees some forty yards below me. It was an interesting experience, for many of the birds when shot fell clear across the river to land on the far bank. Had a hide been built out over the cliff it would have been a perfect example of its kind.

At the time I would have appreciated a fence of some kind, but I have since come to appreciate that this is not something one is likely to find in this country. I gather that in the Swiss and Italian Alpine passes and in the Pyrenees pigeons are shot from hides built out from the cliff side, or edge, when flying through on passage. There may be places in this country where clifftop hides have been constructed for flighting, but I do not personally know of any. When it comes to shooting from quarry or clifftop it is seldom worth bothering with any form of hide. Then the birds are often coming straight over the edge at speed, although there are equally many occasions when they are swerving and curling in the wind far below. A hide is only likely to be required if the birds have been much shot, when a simple strip of camouflage net will probably suffice.

Personal camouflage

From any hide movement, above all, is what attracts the eye of a bird. Movement should be minimal and every consideration given to concealment. This extends to the clothing of the pigeon shooter, which as far as possible should merge with the background. Some enthusiasts go further, draping themselves in dyed nylon curtain material or assuming mobile hides of light garden netting covered with camouflaged material or foliage. This is all very well and such stratagems are often likely to be quite effective, but it is going beyond the normal scope of shooting pigeons over decoys and reverting to the old stalking horse method of shooting.

There is no doubt that such mobile hides, or stalking horses, can be as effective today as in the days of primitive man. It is indeed comparatively simple to make a stalking cow, to match whatever breed is commonest in the area, with the aid of an old sheet sewn onto a cane framework. The framework is simply slotted into a wooden base attached to a rucksack-type of harness. The harness is worn over the shoulders and the sheet painted in matt colouring to resemble a cow, with two 'legs' hanging behind, gives the appearance of the cow's body totally altering the outline of the pigeon shooter. The wood-pigeon sees other cows and expects this to be the same. It does not expect a cow to be a pigeon-shooter and accordingly does not see him, however thin the disguise.

It is really quite unnnecessary, however, for pigeon shooters to experiment with stalking horses, or cows. The normal principles outlined, of investigating the pigeon movements over a much larger area than the shoot itself, then establishing that area's part in the overall pattern, is the first step. The second is preparing hides in the right places and the third is setting out decoys at the right time in the right place and shooting the birds when they come to investigate.

Alternatively the hide may be used for passage shooting, or for shooting birds flighting in to roost. The use of an occasional decoy, especially a decoy lofted in a tree, rather than a number of decoys, may be well worth while here, but on the whole these are different forms of shooting. Nevertheless a good hide has a considerable part to play in both passage shooting and in flighting. In flighting especially, a treetop-level hide comes into its own. Then it truly adds a different dimension to the sport of pigeon shooting.

Finally, when building any sort of hide on any level, make it as roomy as possible. There is nothing worse than trying to shoot in a cramped space. Leave plenty of room to load without tangling with camouflage. Remember you will be spending several hours in it so you may as well be comfortable. Try to make it so that the sun is mostly behind you if possible. In any event do not expose your gun barrels until a bird is well in range and give yourself several good viewing points so that you do not need to bob up and down. Above all, keep still and relax.

7

Various Kinds of Decoys

As with guns, with cartridge making, or hide building, decoys can very easily grow to be of such absorbing interest to the pigeon shooter that they become an end in themselves. There are pigeon shooters who will talk endlessly on making templates for the perfect artificial decoy, or on stuffing birds so that the decoy is better than a real bird and so on. Others are fixated on wing-flapping decoys, or exactly how many birds are required to produce a perfect 'raft', and so on *ad infinitum*. The specialist bore on any subject is always with us.

As with hides, it is worth going back to the earliest use of decoys to define their purpose clearly. Their origins may be lost in the mists of pre-history, but primitive man must have appreciated very early on that tame birds, or beasts, would attract others from the wild. Thus the value of live decoys as a lure to attract birds and beasts from the wild must have been amongst the earliest lessons learned. How long artificial decoys have been used is another matter, but wildfowl decoys have been found in early Egyptian tombs and primitive decoys of mud and feathers were used by Red Indian hunters in North America.

Until it was rightly banned in 1910, along with live pigeon shooting, the use of live birds in the age-old manner was common. Either one or more live birds could be tethered by the leg amongst a number of dead birds set out as if feeding. One at least of these tethered pigeons would have a string attached to its other leg. When he saw any birds flying in the vicinity the waiting gun would twitch this string, causing the tethered bird to flutter its wings, thus attracting the attention of the passing bird to the decoys.

This method of decoying, it must be emphasised, is now rightly illegal. Modern methods, however, emulate in almost every way the principles employed by these Edwardian pigeon shooters. Although today we are restricted to dead or artificial birds as decoys, it is still desirable to emulate, if possible, a bird flapping its wings, as if just changing its position in the flock, like pigeons feeding in the wild. It seems as if the momentary flash of grey and white acts as a natural stimulus on any passing pigeon and causes it, willy nilly, to fly down to investigate.

A shooting acquaintance of mine who lives on the edge of the Pyrenees, where they annually net their steep mountain passes for pigeons migrating through them, told me that they persuade the birds to fly lower into the nets by throwing a white- painted bat across the passes beneath them. Dr R.K.Murton mentions the same fact in his book *The Wood Pigeon.* Probably one side of the bat is white and the other grey so that when twisted with a spinning motion through the air it appears like the flash of a pigeon's wings, acting as an automatic stimulus and causing the bird perforce to drop down to investigate.

Tim Sedgwick, late Editor of *The Shooting Times*, used to argue that he thought pigeons would flight in to iron filings suitably scattered in patches on the ground. The point he was making was that at times pigeons will apparently flight in to almost anything of the right colour in a suitable feeding place. Certainly an old Northumbrian miner friend of mine maintained that he flighted pigeons using nothing more than a grey roof slate with white chalk collar and wing bar markings. The principle is certainly a perfectly sound one.

There is very little argument, however, that the best decoy to set out is a fairly freshly shot dead bird. This, of course, immediately produces a chicken and egg situation, since if the pigeon shooter has no dead birds to use as decoys he is not in a position to shoot birds. In such circumstances, if the pigeon shooter is not in a position to go out the night before and shoot sufficient birds to act as the initial decoys, there is nothing for it but to fall back on artificial substitutes.

There are quite a few different types of artificial decoys available and before discussing the various different kinds it is as well to consider what the decoy is supposed to be doing. A decoy, of any kind, is present as a lure to bring birds or animals of its kind within range of the hunter. The principal lures are sex and food. In this case food is the major factor used to encourage the pigeon to come to the decoys. There is, too, the fact that the pigeon is a gregarious bird, liking to travel and eat in flocks, and the intention of the decoy or decoys is also to appeal to this natural instinct. There is thus probably an element of sex involved as well.

The grey colouring of the wood-pigeon's body and the white of the neck ring and wing bands are important features in decoying the birds since they stand out at a considerable distance and serve to attract attention, or alternatively may appear as a warning signal. The flash of the white wing bands when a bird flaps its wings as it flies briefly to the front of the flock is often enough to attract the attention of a passing bird to the grey of the mass of birds feeding. It is necessary therefore for any decoys to be of the correct colour of grey and preferably to show white neck bands and white wing bands. The approaching bird is likely to notice very quickly if there is anything wrong with the colour of artificial decoys set out for it.

The importance of using a flat matt paint on the decoys rather than a glossy shiny grey, or white, cannot be over-emphasised. Any decoys which are the wrong colour will cause approaching birds to shy away at once. Similarly the birds should be set out in a life-like way, approaching the behaviour of birds in the wild. It is well worth taking a pair of binoculars for a day or two and simply studying the feeding habits of wild birds until their attitudes and behaviour are clear in the mind. It will be noted that they tend to move steadily in a flock, the pattern of which may alter depending on the ground, wind and weather conditions. When it comes to setting out decoys it is important to imitate the habits of the wild birds as nearly as possible.

Natural decoys

If the pigeon shooter cannot obtain newly shot birds as decoys the problem remains of finding the most desirable substitute to start the day. If he lives in a town and cannot readily get out the day before to shoot birds to act as decoys it is always possible to keep half-a-dozen or more birds in the deep freeze ready for action when required. It is important, however, to put them in the freezer in the shape it is desired to use them, as initially when taken out they will be frozen solid. Once they start to thaw, of course, their heads must be propped up with a wood or wire tealer in the usual way.

The snag with using frozen birds is that it usually tends to be an expensive way of decoying as they can be used only once. Another lot of birds should then be kept back for the next occasion. After a hot summer's day they will probably be fit only to throw away; after a winter's day they may be edible, but it is unlikely a game dealer would take them. It is possible they might be re-frozen and used again but it would be courting food poisoning to eat them and they would have to be thrown away eventually. For the town gun, who cannot get out to shoot birds as decoys in advance, the only real alternative to using artificial decoys would seem to be buying some dead birds from a butcher, but in that case why not go a step further, save on cartridges and buy fifty birds, then call it a day?

There are, of course, those who will not be satisfied with shooting birds the night before, or using some of the better types of manufactured decoys. A.E.B. Johnson in his book *Shooting Wood-Pigeon*, published in 1961 by Herbert

Jenkins, recommended trying amateur taxidermy, skinning and curing one's own birds to make decoys. His suggestions were remarkably close to those advocated a decade or so later by a Surgeon Commander Cleave in an article in *The Field*. This method was adopted by The Wildfowler's Association of Great Britain and Ireland, or WAGBI, as it was then termed.(Now, of course, The British Association for Conservation and Shooting, or BASC.) Anyone who wishes to have exact details on this method of what amounts to embalming birds should apply to BASC headquarters for full particulars. It is a way of making decoys that is only likely to appeal to someone with a medical background, or with leanings that way.

Briefly, the method involves using a diluted solution of formaldehyde, or formalin, which can be obtained from chemists, but requires rubber gloves when using it. Another requirement is a hypodermic syringe, and disposable plastic syringes can usually be obtained easily enough from vets, when the purpose is explained. Otherwise the routine is slightly less tricky than that described by Johnson. He suggested skinning the bird. In this method the bird is laid on its back and split down the breastbone with a sharp knife. The meat is removed for eating, then the legs and feet are cut off. The intestines are all removed, then, without breaking the skin of the back a gap is cut in the spine to allow for insertion of a wire which is doubled over and thrust into the skull to support the corpse in a lifelike stance. A solution of formalin is injected into the ends of the wings and wing joints and also the skull. The entire body cavity is swabbed out with the solution, then stuffed with cotton wool and sewn up tightly with a needle and thread, leaving a loop of the wire outside as a carrying handle and stand. It is argued that with practice it only takes some twenty minutes a bird and they are supposed to last for up to two years.

The snag with all these decoys is that they do not readily stand up to hard wear. Even when sprayed with hair lacquer to keep the feathers in reasonable condition they still have to be carefully packed for carrying and if too much formaldehyde is used they can become very brittle and easily broken. In my view this is carrying the business of making decoys into the same realm as gun collecting mania. If you want to shoot pigeons, stick to shooting pigeons, not stuffing them. If you want to stuff them, become a taxidermist.

To be fair it must be admitted that even freshly shot dead birds have disadvantages on occasions. In hot weather for instance, even if sprayed with insect repellent, they can very easily become fly blown. The same is also naturally the case with any freshly shot birds used to make up the 'raft' of decoys, even when they too are sprayed with insect repellent. Of course, those in favour of taxidermy in one form or another will probably quite rightly make the very valid point that flies are unlikely to worry their products unless they have been badly finished. This is almost certainly the case since formaldehyde is probably every bit as effective as the very best insect repellent invented. It is poisonous, has a particularly unpleasant, penetrating smell and stains very badly. However, one other advantage might be claimed for this type of decoy in that even the stupidest gundog is unlikely to make the mistake of retrieving one of them, or if he does, he is only going to do so once.

Artificial decoys

There is no particular reason beyond personal preference why the pigeon shooter should use dead birds initially instead of artificial decoys. While dead birds, if artistically set out, are inevitably more like the live pigeon, some artificial decoys are extremely effective. Many experienced pigeon shooters will have seen offers of mating approaches made to artificial decoys by other pigeons and also attacks initiated by passing hawks. Thus, in some cases anyway, their resemblance to nature would appear to be good enough for all practical purposes.

In the past decade the market has been flooded with continental products, some of which are extremely good and some of which are useless. Many of the modern artificial decoys are made of moulded polymer, or similar material, which is light and tough. Slightly larger than life, which is probably a good thing anyway, since the attention of the passing pigeon is more readily attracted, these are especially good as lofted decoys. They have a hook under the tail so that half a dozen can be linked onto a length of cord or wire. They have a small loop on the back so that they can be hung from a nylon fishing line, if so required, for lofting. They also have a very sensible hole in the base in which a cane can be inserted, either to stand them in a field, or for lofting. These are as good as any decoy and reasonably cheap. Half-a-dozen are a useful standby for any serious pigeon shooter.

A possible improvement on these is the flat silhouette version in the same material, which has a simple turn bar which spreads the silhouette out into a quite presentable plump bird. The advantage of these is that a number can be carried flat more easily and take up much less room than the full-bodied decoys. Despite the awkwardness of the latter, however, it is undoubtedly more lifelike and on balance is probably preferable.

Most experienced pigeon shooters will have acquired or made numerous decoys over the years. On the whole any rubber or rubberised decoys are best avoided. They may be good initially, but they tend to perish over the years and require careful storage and carriage, so that they are not really to be recommended, even if they are still available. This also goes for the inflatable type, although these tend to be more effective and look more lifelike.

The simple Max Baker cut-out type of decoy still has its devotees. This is a light cut-out model of a pigeon made from a simple template, on stiff paper, linoleum, tin, or any similar light material easily cut and glued, riveted, or soldered. The result is a hollow shell decoy, which stacks one inside another for easy carriage. Painted a matt grey with the suitable white ring neck and wing bars it still makes a useful decoy. The important feature of any Max Baker type decoy is the correct centering of the hole for the peg on which it should be mounted, about level with the shoulders. The originals had a hole in the centre of the back and a bent metal tab underneath, which allowed the decoy a tilting movement in the wind but stopped it turning round and pointing the wrong way.

There are several modern variants on the Max Baker idea, but whether they are any improvement is another matter. One of these is a light cardboard version which has a colour photograph of a feeding pigeon viewed from above printed on it. In any sort of wind these are liable to blow away and they are not likely to last long in wet weather, but are probably good enough when the sun is shining and conditions are suitable for them. Rather stronger, but even lighter, is another version in extremely light celluloid known as a 'Shell' decoy. These have a plastic-topped peg which fits into a hole in the back and allows them to tilt in the wind, but supposedly prevents them blowing away. Although these do not appear to look much like pigeons, being shaped more like a moulded plastic toy, they can be surprisingly effective. In windy conditions, however, they are likely to take off and ruin the proceedings as the pigeon shooter chases them round the field. They are also not likely to last long as they are liable to crack if squashed in a game bag, or underfoot.

Flat silhouette outlines of a bird, as with wild geese silhouettes, can be perfectly effective and are probably preferable to some of the other alternatives. The fact of the matter is, as Tim Sedgwick used to argue, that very nearly anything in the right colours will prove effective when placed in the right place at the right time. My old miner friend's method with a slate stuck upright in the ground and marked with chalk was probably perfectly sound, even if carrying a number of heavy slates around may not have been such a good idea.

Further modifications

There are other systems of improving on what the manufacturers or Nature have contrived. One favourite is to glue pigeon wings, or feathers, onto decoys. There are also those who recommend that a bird be skinned and treated with formaldehyde, then placed over a rubber decoy with the head removed. The head of the bird, duly treated with formaldehyde, is then thrust into the hole left in the neck. In some ways this is probably a sounder plan than using an embalmed bird, in that it is tougher and more easily handled, but even these decoys have to be treated with care.

The big advantage of polymer decoys is that they can be thrown about with impunity in the way decoys almost inevitably are manhandled. If each time the decoys are handled the pigeon shooter has to remind himself that they involved hours of work he is bound to be slower and more inhibited about getting them quickly into position. There are, however, obviously people who like decoys for themselves alone. The acid question is, do these enthusiasts shoot more pigeons as a result, or would they be better employed in some other way?

Basically, decoys should be lifelike; they should be easy to handle; easy to carry and quick to set out. They should not be unduly affected by wind or weather. On all these counts the polymer decoys mentioned are very nearly perfect and it certainly has to be admitted that pigeon decoying has greatly improved since the days before the last war when solid decoys, hand-carved by local experts, were to be found in many country gunshops. The weight alone of these solid wooden decoys must have militated against their use, but no doubt the pigeons were not quite so sophisticated in those days.

The next advance will presumably be a silicon chip and battery powered motor inside a polymer dummy which will walk around, peck the ground, spread its wings and possibly even call out to passing pigeons. No doubt even

Decoys set out in line. From the front: dead feral bird: rubber decoy: polymer decoy: wing flapping polymer decoy.

then there will be those who insist that the chip and motor should be inserted in a stuffed bird. There is, however, really nothing to stop anyone making such a decoy, but where should the line be drawn? Science used in such a way to copy and outwit Nature is totally unforgiveable. Like tape recordings of wildfowl used to draw them within range of the gun, this would have to be made illegal.

Wing-flapping decoys

Having made this point it is, however, not unreasonable to use various comparatively primitive methods to introduce movement amongst the decoys to attract the attention of passing birds. A bird thrown by a wingtip at the right moment to provide the necessary glimpse of white wing bars can attract the attention of a passing bird and be enough to cause it to turn towards the decoys. This is the same principle used by the netters in the Pyrenees. It would appear there is almost certainly something compulsive about a pigeon's reaction to the stimulus of seeing these colours in movement.

The methods employed to produce the effect of movement range from simply throwing a dead bird, through fairly primitive wing- flapping decoys worked by strong nylon line, to quite sophisticated models. There are at present several types of wing-flapping decoys which can be bought. Most of them are reasonably effective, allowing the decoy to be set out some distance from the hide and the wings to be operated by a nylon line when needed. The basic requirement is that the stick supporting the decoy is firmly embedded in the ground so that, when the nylon line is pulled, the decoy is not overturned. If the line is given three or four quick tugs this is enough to move the wings up and down several times and should attract the attention of the passing bird.

An improvement is the use of a dead bird, for it is quite simple to peg out a dead bird with both wings broken at the shoulder. A nylon line attached to each wing tip is then led through a hole in the top of a wire stake set in the ground level with each wing. These lines are joined together a yard or so away and a single line led off to the hide. When required, the pigeon shooter jerks the line four or five times and the wings are automatically flapped.

What was originally called the WAGBI/Semark wing-flapper, now the BASC/Semark wing-flapper, named after the inventor, a Mr Semark and marketed by the BASC headquarters, works very efficiently. The dead bird is set into a cradle with the wings broken at the shoulder joints. When the nylon line is jerked the effect is realistic and can draw birds well. There is at least one other wing-flapping device available on the market but there is still scope for the do-it-yourself enthusiast to have a field day.

8

Decoys on Various Levels

Depending on the type of decoy chosen from the varieties already discussed there will be different methods required for setting them out. Almost every decoy requires some form of stick, stand or support, to set it out in the most lifelike manner possible. In general the sticks provided with most artificial decoys are highly inadequate, frequently being painted white, or some such ludicrous colour, apart from being so badly made that they snap when first used. It is almost always worth checking any such wooden or wire supports provided with decoys and replacing them with one's own where required.

Where using dead birds as decoys it is desirable to use either a simple 6-8 in.-long sharpened wooden stick, or length of stiffish wire, as a tealer which can be thrust into the ground and up through the crop and neck of the bird into the base of the skull to support the head in a lifelike position. A neatly trimmed forked stick can be used unobtrusively to support the neck and head in the same From the point of view of simplicity such tealers are best made of wood. If these are overlooked when picking up the decoys at the end of the day, the loss is unimportant. Although in some ways easier to use, a piece of wire is not such a desirable item to leave in a field where it may be trodden on, swallowed by grazing stock, or stick in the blades of a combine or other machinery. On the whole, however, either wood or wire tealers are simple and quick to use when setting up dead birds as decoys and are easy to carry, taking up very little space.

A cradle may be very readily made on the model put

forward by Charles Coles in his book *Shooting Pigeons* published in *The Shooting Times* library series in 1964. This was a three-pronged cradle with short metal prongs on either side to hold the body of the bird under the wings with a longer prong forward thrust in under the bird's throat to support the head in a natural position. To raise a decoy above crops, or for use with a lofted decoy, this cradle was doubtless effective enough. The bird lay in it, clasped firmly in position rather like an egg in an eggcup.

A similar type of cradle can easily be constructed from a wire coathanger twisted into shape. With a rubber band holding the bird in position this can also be used as a lofted decoy. Since this is one of the few uses for old wire coathangers the suggestion is passed on for what it is worth. It is effective enough, but the cradle itself is just another item of equipment to be mislaid at the end of the day and it is certainly not a desirable thing to leave lying around a field.

Having considered the various decoys available to attract pigeons within range of his hide and made his choice, the next important decision for the pigeon shooter is how to set them out in the best way to attract the birds. It is essential when considering where to put the decoys to remember that all birds automatically turn into the wind to land. This will inevitably have a considerable bearing on where the decoys are placed in relation to the hide. With skilled positioning of the decoys relative to the hide, the experienced pigeon shooter should be able to cause incoming birds to flight into the flock more or less exactly where he wishes, so as to present him with a simple shot in a pre-determined killing zone.

Siting the decoys

There are various ways the decoys can be set out to achieve this, but much depends on the circumstances, the ground, the hide and the surroundings. No two occasions will be exactly alike, even successive days on the same ground when conditions appear identical, but there are usually certain principles which can be applied successfully. For instance, although pigeons may at first sight seem to be feeding in an unco-ordinated and unplanned mass, a little careful observation will show that, as with all birds, there is a form of pecking order. In general, any birds joining the flock will do so from behind and flight in towards the rear of the main body of birds. The general etiquette of flock behaviour seems to dictate that newcomers fly in towards the rear of the flock, or any suitable open space towards the rear where the birds are feeding. In conjunction with the fact that the pigeon will alight into the wind, such behaviour can be utilised when the pigeon shooter is setting out his decoys.

Once the field in which the pigeons are feeding has been identified and the flight lines being used to approach it have been noted, the next step is to decide on where to place the hide. If the preliminary reconnaissance has been carried out successfully it may be that a ready-made hide is already in position. Otherwise it will be necessary to make one in the most suitable spot near where the birds have been feeding. Once the hide has been constructed, it is then necessary to set out the decoys so that approaching birds flighting in to them present themselves favourably to the waiting gun. Here the wind direction is the most important factor, although the nature of the ground and the crop on which they are feeding also affect the issue.

Looking at the situation of the hide in relation to the ground and the wind the first point is to decide on the best and most suitable killing zone. From that stems the decision as to where to place the decoys. With that area in mind they must be slightly upwind from that point, say twenty to thirty yards up wind of the hide. They may thus be either right or left of the hide, or where the wind is blowing straight at the hide, some twenty or thirty yards out into the field. If the wind is blowing from behind the hide it may be necessary to move the birds nearer to the hide itself.

As well as their placing in relation to the wind and the hide, the way the decoys are set out will also have its effect in bringing the birds into the desired area. Thus the decoys may be set out in two slightly separate groups with the effect that birds tend to flight into the space between the two groups. Alternatively they may be placed in the form of a slight inverted U, with the curve away from the hide so that the incoming birds tend to flight into the centre of the U. In the same way a half-U can be used to encourage birds to flight into the tempting curl at the end. From any of these initial groups a larger flock can be built up effectively. Thus two small groups, each slightly half-U-shaped, can be turned easily into a larger U-shaped single group as it is built up and an initial half-U-shape can be turned into a full U-shape by degrees. If the wind is from behind the hide the curve of the U may be towards the pigeon shooter.

The mechanics of a wing-flapping decoy have already been discussed, but its placing is another matter. Where such a decoy can be lofted, if only on a fence post, its value may well be greatly increased. If it is on the ground with the other decoys it should be near the tail end of the flock, within reasonably easy reach of the pigeon shooter so that the nylon line used to activate it does not have to be too long. The line should also, of course, lead direct from the hide to the device to avoid any hitches when using it. If so placed, when the wings are flapped quickly two or three times it will give the appearance to any passing pigeon of having just landed behind the flock.

Starting with an initial half-dozen or dozen birds as decoys the flock can be gradually built up to some twenty to thirty, but once the birds are coming successfully there is little point in continuing to build up an ever larger raft of decoys. From the first, however, it always worth thinking of having decoys as far as possible on various levels. This is especially the case, for instance, when shooting over laid corn, or crops such as peas. Here especially it is worth having several decoys raised on bamboo poles or on netting laid on top of the crop itself, while the rest are on the ground. The decoys are thus likely to be very much more visible from a distance to passing birds.

In any event, whatever the ground or the crop on which the decoys are set out, it is always worth trying to put out a lofted decoy within range. Where there is a likely tree close at hand in which pigeons might be expected to perch, especially something with a few dead branches bare of foliage, a lofted decoy can often prove a very considerable draw. Where no such tree is available it is always worth considering putting a pigeon on top of a fence post. Such a decoy, although not very high above ground, still constitutes a lofted decoy and can be visible from a surprising distance. Again this can prove a very effective draw, attracting passing birds who may initially be drawn by the sight of the single bird, then see the flock and flight in to join them. Alternatively they may sometimes flight into the same tree as a lofted decoy rather than join the flock, hence it is as well always to be within range of any such decoy.

Just as it is advisable whenever possible to vary the levels on which the decoys are placed, by having at least one lofted decoy, so it is always desirable to vary the decoys themselves. It is seldom that one sees a flock of wood-pigeons without at least one feral bird attached to it, or for that matter a flock of feral birds without one wood-pigeon. The two are completely compatible and the sight of a flock of either will be sufficient to attract species of both. It is even probable that a mixed flock is more common in many areas and more attractive to either species. Where it is easier to obtain feral birds there is no objection to using them in preference to wood-pigeons as the initial decoys; it appears to make no difference to results.

Presenting the decoys

Having decided on the siting of the hide, where to place
the decoys and roughly in what pattern they should best
be set out, the next step is to set them up in as lifelike
a way as possible. There is a great deal of nonsense talked
about exact spacing and how much distance should be left

*Lofting a decoy in a prominent position in a hedgerow, where
a ditch makes a convenient natural hide.*

between birds and so on. Much of this probably stems from
the decoy fetishists who have prepared each bird with
meticulous care and are prepared to spend valuable time
setting them out with mathematical precision. They may
get results, but lobbing the birds out from the game bag,
or sack, in the direction it has been decided to put them
and then setting them up roughly where they land, is likely
to be equally successful. As long as some attempt at a
planned pattern is maintained the exact distances between
birds are best left to chance. In any flock the birds are likely
to be spaced more or less haphazardly as each attacks its
own area of feeding, one moment quite close to another
bird and some moments later a yard or so away.

The next important task is to set the birds up in a lifelike
way, using tealers of wood or wire, or cradles, as preferred.
For a start it is desirable that they should not all be set
out in exactly the same manner. They should obviously
not all have their heads held high, for such a pose indicates
a flock that is alarmed and is about to take flight. Any
approaching bird seeing all the heads raised in this way,
would automatically take fright and jinx away. Some birds
should be set out with heads down, some with heads up,
and they should not by any means all be facing
regimentally in the same direction or neatly spaced like
guardsmen on parade. Any such regimentation, or total
regularity, is to be strictly avoided for as every countryman
knows Nature abhors regularity of this kind.

Lofted decoys

As noted earlier, one or more lofted decoys are often useful
when flighting pigeons in to roost. This is especially so
when shooting from a platform, where a well placed lofted
decoy can attract the attention of birds flighting in and
bring them within easy range of the gun. Decoys for
flighting are more important, of course, when shooting
from a hide either at treetop level or below, rather than
when shooting in a clearing or in a ride in the wood, where

it is possible to move around if it is seen that birds are not coming in that particular direction.

The actual lofting of a decoy is not always an easy matter. Various methods are usually recommended, from the use of a chimney sweep's rods, special lofting canes, or light bamboo rods fitting into each other in the same manner, to using a line thrown over a tree branch so that the dummy can be hauled into position. The snag with the last method is that a bare branch within easy throwing distance is not always available, or where available, not always suitable for the purpose.

Some interesting alternatives have been airily advocated for this latter method from time to time. These range from throwing a cricket ball with the line attached (which is by no means always as easy as it sounds, inside a wood); shooting a line over with a bow and arrow; and using a casting rod and line. The obvious drawbacks, that not everyone is proficient with bows and arrows, or casting rods, and that this means more equipment to carry, are enough to discount these suggestions. The fact remains that any such method can easily end with a weight tangled round a branch well up a tree and consequent loss of temper.

Using a sweep's poles, or specially made extending poles, can work well, but there is a limit to the height even they will reach without swaying perilously and bending, or even breaking. The same limitations affect the use of bamboo poles. If the bamboo lengths are not long enough an aluminium ladder can be useful. Even then any decoy, whether artificial or a dead bird in a cradle, requires at least the steadying weight of a bamboo pole below it. It is a good idea to tape a lead weight to the base of the pole to steady the decoy and keep it in position head into the wind as it should be naturally. Where the decoy is suspended from a nylon line it will be necessary to suspend a weight beneath it to stop it swaying unduly in the wind, or another line may be required to anchor it firmly to the ground.

Observing behaviour

It is always worth studying the reaction of the first approaching birds which appear likely to flight in to the flock of decoys. If they flight right in without any hesitation then clearly everything is satisfactory. If they start to come in and then jinx away abruptly it means either that they have seen something suspicious about the decoys, or that they have spotted the pigeon shooter in his hide. If the next birds approaching react in the same way and the pigeon shooter is certain there is nothing wrong with the hide and that he made no giveaway movement, then it is as well to inspect the decoys quickly to see if there is anything the matter with them.

Anything unusual or unnatural about the decoys will be enough to cause an approaching bird to jinx away. It may be that one or two have fallen over, or that some shot birds have not been picked. Alternatively some may be obviously wrongly placed, pointing downwind, or unduly regimented or some other such glaring mistake. It does not take a great deal out of the ordinary to attract the attention of approaching birds and frighten them away. Until the cause has been discovered and eliminated it is unlikely the pigeon shooter will have much success. It is thus always worth checking over the decoys at any time if several birds in succession are seen to turn away unexpectedly.

If artificial decoys are used initially, or, as is often the case, a mixture of both artificial and dead birds, it is sometimes suggested that the artificial decoys should be replaced by freshly shot birds. If reliance can be placed in the artificial decoys, however, there is surely no need to remove them and the test must be whether birds are coming into them without detecting them. If they are doing so, such unnecessary replacement merely suggests a lack of confidence on the part of the pigeon shooter.

9

Points to Note

Assuming all is going well and pigeons are flighting into the decoys laid out for them, there are certain points to remember. If two birds come in more or less together it is as well to let the first come right in and take the second as it approaches, then take the other as it flies off. To take the first as it comes in would mean the second jinxing away at the shot and possibly being missed.

When shooting on a hot sunny day remember to carry an anti-fly spray, not merely for your own benefit. Whenever birds are shot and being set up as decoys, a quick spray will help to keep the flies away from them and prevent them becoming fly-blown before being picked up when the day is over. The spray will also help the dog to distinguish between birds to be retrieved and those to be left, although he will know by the scent when his master has handled a bird which he should then leave alone. It is, however, a good plan to let the dog have his own spy hole from the hide so that he can mark the fall of each bird.

If the pigeons just are not coming in, do not sit wasting your time and refusing to admit that you have made a mistake. The commonest error, but none the less infuriating, is when you find you have misjudged the place they are coming into a large field. It may be that you have only mistaken the flight line by a hundred and fifty yards, but as a result the birds are clearly feeding at the other end of the field with only a few veering across to show interest in your decoys. There is no point in being stubborn about it as that will not result in more pigeons. Make the best of a bad job and move as soon as possible to a more suitable hide. Then try to work out the reasons for the mistake. Was it that you took the wrong tree as a marker from a distance, or misjudged through binoculars where the birds were flying? Or is it merely that this side of the field has been eaten out and they have moved on? It always pays to try to learn from one's mistakes and work out the reasons so as to avoid them in future.

It may just be that your timing was wrong. In the winter the birds are feeding most of the day because the hours of daylight are shorter. Then it should be possible to tell fairly soon whether they are going to come into the decoys, or are feeding elsewhere. In the spring through to the autumn the days are longer and the cover tends to be thicker so that it is not always so easy to see the feeding birds. They also tend to feed later and earlier, so that there may be a lull during the middle of the day when they are digesting the morning's intake. This is very much the case in the summer months, and after the early morning feed there may be a lull of several hours until they start feeding again in the afternoon and continue until about six o'clock in the evening. As always it is a question of keeping the eyes open and using the binoculars to identify the flight lines to the major feeding places.

The weather can also have a considerable effect on the movement of birds. Pigeons do not like feeding in rain and tend to stay under cover. The threat of snow will also make pigeons stay put, like most wild birds or beasts. Fog will again force them to stay close to their roosts, and a mixture of snow and mist will have much the same effect. This is not to say that they cannot be shot in such conditions, but rather that decoying then is liable to be a waste of time. Clearly, for instance, putting out decoys in fog or heavy mist can only be regarded as an act of lunacy. In such circumstances, however, they may be shot in roosting woods as they tend to remain close to the familiar ground they know best. In very hot weather they may be found at favourite watering places and a decoy or two in such situations may bring in a steady number of birds at intervals over a few hours.

One point is worth making regarding shooting over laid crops. Where a crop is badly laid, do not make matters worse by walking around in it either to set up decoys or to pick up dead birds. Try as far as possible to set up the decoys to the side of the damaged area so that shot birds will fall outside it and may be picked up without causing further damage. If birds do fall in standing crops it is better to leave them than risk ruining what the pigeons have left.

While in general pigeon shooting is a solitary sport, it is often possible to have two or three guns working together intelligently to keep birds moving in a way which benefits them all. Having set up one gun with decoys under the incoming flight line near where the birds are feeding, another gun may be set up under the outgoing flight line in the same field to take any birds disturbed by the first.

If a third gun can then find the assembly area where the pigeons are collecting before and after feeding they may all have good sport, although the gun on the outgoing flight line may have fewer birds than the others.

When it comes to flighting birds in to roost, or dawn flighting, this principle can be worked to good effect with several guns, depending, of course, on the ground. A lot too may depend on the wind. If there is little or no wind, as with duck flighting, the birds may tend to circle high and sideslip into their chosen roosting places. This does not mean there will be no shooting, but merely that it will be much more difficult than when the birds are forced by a good strong breeze to flight in around treetop level. Then, if they are well organised, there will be every chance for several guns to have good sport.

In such circumstances, as with decoying, it is essential to remain flexible. Do not be afraid to move fifty or sixty yards in one direction or another until you have found a good flight line. This can make all the difference to having a good or merely indifferent day. If your first position is unsatisfactory and you can see pigeons flighting in regularly some fifty yards away, then by all means go to the pigeons, for it is perfectly plain they are not going to

A good stand at the edge of a clearing waiting for birds flighting in to roost.

come to you. One or two pigeons may fly in your direction, but if by moving you can get amongst them then move along as soon as you are sure of your facts.

If you are taking part in an organised pigeon shoot and have been put in position by the organiser, however, it is not advisable to wander too far from where you are placed. This is largely a matter of tact. There are likely to be good reasons why the spot was chosen and by moving too far you may be upsetting his overall plans. In such circumstances it is wise to check, before the shoot starts, how far you may be allowed to move or whether you are expected to stay put.

On such occasions, as when shooting from a platform, a dog is extremely useful. A good experienced marker who heads for the crash of the bird through the trees, retrieving automatically, is worth a great deal. If he brings to hand only those birds which are still alive and gets on with the job of retrieving on his own without further orders he is invaluable in this sort of shooting. Although this may not be approved Field Trial practice, that is by the way. The dog is required in this case to do a specialised job of work and without him your bag is likely to be much smaller, for it is certain that if you have to retrieve your own birds you will lose numerous opportunities of shooting others. On the other hand if you do not retrieve them at once you are likely to lose track of where they fell and thus inevitably fail to pick some of them as darkness approaches.

A point to bear in mind on such occasions is that it is desirable to finish shooting at a reasonable hour. It is surprisingly true that shooting of this nature, especially from treetop platforms, does not seem to disturb game and that pheasants will go to roost quite close while guns are still blazing away. The fact remains that the landowner, his gamekeeper, or the shoot organiser is liable to feel worried about the effects of such shooting unless it is deliberately organised so as to drive birds into home ground. In any event it is always as well to stop while birds

Retrieving from the quarry floor is not always an easy task for the dog.

are still coming in so that they will not desert the area. It is worth therefore halting while it is still light enough to see clearly, even if there seems to be an endless stream of birds still coming in to roost.

There are other good reasons for calling a halt while it is still light. One is that you will still have time in daylight to pick your birds and this applies especially, of course, to those who do not have a dog with them. You will also have time to collect all your gear, including any lofted decoys, and carry it to the car. A sackful of over fifty pigeons can add a considerable weight to all your other paraphernalia, even if your cartridge bag may be significantly lighter.

If you have any distance to walk it is also desirable to have some light while negotiating your way over unfamiliar barbed wire fences, ditches, or ploughed fields. To attempt this in the dark, especially when weighed down with a heavy load, is not the most enjoyable of pastimes. It is an almost certain way of losing something, if only your temper. In such circumstances it will be appreciated why it is preferable to be able to bring the car/van/land-rover close to the place where you are shooting.

With the return to your car at long last it is important to remember that the day is by no means finished. There may be various presents of birds to pass on to farmers or farmworkers who have been helpful. These should first be cropped, if only for your own benefit, to check on what they have been feeding and to ensure that they are cleared of any green feeding. Then there is the gun to be cleaned and the dog to be looked after, and if necessary fed and bedded on your return.

It is also desirable to hang the birds up separately in a well ventilated fly-proof larder after emptying and inspecting their crops. In hot weather the birds should also be examined to make sure they are not fly-blown and where there are any eggs these should be wiped off with a damp cloth. It is amazing what a difference to the edibility of the birds a little elementary care of this nature will make. If they are just left in a sack overnight the chances are that by morning they will only be fit for ferrets. To waste a day's time and effort in this way is foolish.

The same rule of giving up before it becomes dark applies equally to cliff or quarry shooting. There is no point whatever in disturbing birds to such an extent that they depart elsewhere. Nor are cliffs or quarries ideal places to linger around when darkness is falling. Of course, the tide tables dictate the timing of any cliff shooting, but it is always advisable to bear in mind how the tides relate to the hours of daylight. It is also advisable when cliff shooting to allow more time than has been initially estimated when as it is easy to find oneself held up for longer than one expects when, for instance, retrieving a bird which has fallen in an awkward place.

If there is any danger of being caught by darkness in whatever form of shooting, whether over decoys, flighting birds in to roost, or by cliff or quarry, a torch can always be extremely useful. For checking on equipment as darkness is falling a torch can be invaluable. Even a small standby pocket torch is worth carrying whenever there is any chance of being caught by darkness, especially in tricky country such as the quarry or cliff edge. There are times when it can literally prove a life saver.

There is one other form of pigeon shooting which has not been mentioned so far and that is shooting feral pigeons roosting in farm buildings or ruins. There can be few farms, especially those which store grain in bulk, where there are not some feral pigeons permanently roosting on the premises. Such feral birds are also usually to be found in any ruined buildings, or isolated barns and outhouses. Although most farmers are resigned to the presence of a few such birds around their farms they can frequently become a considerable nuisance, fouling both machinery and feed. In general, however, they are not easy birds to discourage since a ready source of food is at hand.

The difficulty of shooting such birds with a twelve-bore is that they very quickly appreciate its potential danger. After being shot at a few times they become extremely wary, clearing off after the first shot, or even at the sight of anyone with a gun. There is also the difficulty that where there is stock around it is usually undesirable to fire a twelve-bore too close to them. This can be potentially very dangerous around a farm. Animals that are pregnant may lose their young, or injure themselves if frightened by the unexpected sound of the gun.

One alternative in such circumstances may be a .410 and for some buildings it may be the answer. When pigeons are seen to be getting out of control a .410 is often used in cases where a twelve-bore might cause alarm, for instance in public parks or cemeteries or in many of the country's ruins when closed to the public. However, even the .410 has its shortcomings since it cannot be fired inside many buildings with safety and its range is another limiting factor.

The ideal weapon inside a building, or at close range on birds perched on suitable places such as roof trees, or crow-stepped gable ends is an air rifle. A .177, or .22 air rifle can be used most effectively against pigeons both inside and outside farm buildings with little danger of any damage being done to anything other than the pigeons. The fact that it is silent in operation is its biggest advantage.

Once again, as in any form of pigeon shooting, reconnaissance is necessary before setting to work. It should be carefully noted where the birds tend to roost. When their favourite places have been spotted, it is then necessary to find a good vantage point within range from which the area can be covered. Some form of hide may need to be built, but often it is just a question of moving a straw bale from a stack or opening a skylight a little for the pigeon shooter. In this way even a youngster can make some surprisingly large bags in quite a short time.

As a means of introducing youngsters to pigeon shooting and decoying this can be as good as any. If it is explained what they must do, they can make the preliminary reconnaissance themselves and decide on the most likely spots for shooting the pigeons. If desired, a decoy can be lofted in a suitable position, but it is usually unnecessary. On one farm to which I have access I set down a young cousin aged sixteen and left him to his own devices. In the morning he returned with sixty birds after two and a half hours and in the afternoon he bettered his performance with seventy feral pigeons, all cleanly shot. His only misadventure was when he dropped one inside the bull pen and wisely decided not to try to retrieve it. Despite this mayhem there seemed as many birds as ever round the farm steading just a week later.

Blood and Feathers

My wife, who is a superlative cook, tends sometimes to refer rather sourly to the shooting season as being just 'mud, blood and feathers'. From certain angles one can see her point, even if like so many culinary near-truths this is an over-simplification. It is obviously not much fun having to pluck and draw, or skin and gut sundry beasts from snipe to deer before cooking them, especially if you have had none of the excitement and satisfaction involved in the hunt. It behoves every reasonable shooting man with any claim to a sense of decency therefore to make sure that this side of the task is dealt with by him and not left to his wife.

To start with it is important to hang all birds and beasts (and this includes pigeons, despite what some people may say to the contrary) in a suitably fly-proof larder. Assuming that your pigeons have had the contents of their crops removed soon after being brought back and that they have been hung so as to allow the air to circulate freely round them, the next step is to prepare them for cooking. Unless you propose to roast them or casserole them whole, it is generally quite unnecessary to pluck them, since all that is really required is the breast meat and it is a simple operation to skin the breast, remove it and dispose of the carcase.

Pigeons are the simplest of birds to pluck and the process, if necessary, should not take more than a couple of minutes. A useful tip when plucking birds is to plunge them briefly into very hot water before starting. The feathers will then come away very quickly. Pigeons are so simple, however, that the only advantage of this is to stop the feathers spreading far and wide.

If it is desired merely to remove the breast meat the answer is to work beside a sizeable sink, on a large flat draining board with a large bowl or bucket of water on one side and a waste-bin with plastic liner open on the other. The pile of pigeons to be dealt with should be lying on the draining board with a free flat space available. A very sharp pointed knife is the essential tool.

Lay the first pigeon on its back. Draw the knife down the breastbone, just piercing the skin. Draw the skin back with the thumbs and forefingers on either side, thus divesting the bird of its feathered waistcoat. Run the knife down one side of the breastbone as close as possible and ease off that side of breast meat, regardless of feathers adhering to it, and drop the piece of meat into the bowl or bucket of water. Then deal with the other side in the same way and dispose of the carcase in the waste bin. Start on the next, then the next, and the next, and so on. Finally it is necessary to go over the breasts in the bowl or bucket and remove any surplus feathers by holding the meat under the cold tap. It is surprising how quick it is possible to become at this method of dealing with pigeons.

Whether using the entire bird, or merely the breasts, it is always worth picking out the young birds. Since you will in any case get a better price from any game dealer for your old birds if you are selling them, this makes eminently good sense. Young feral birds or collared doves, which are both anyway classified as small birds by game dealers and accordingly do not fetch such a good price, are particularly good eating. In this respect pigeons are the opposite of game birds where, of course, the young command a better price as being more tender and better eating. Making a virtue of necessity therefore, you may as well keep only the best young plump birds for your personal consumption.

Assuming that you have on hand a supply of plump young pigeons' breasts you have the basis for a number of extremely mouth-watering dishes. With the exercise of a little imagination there is virtually no end to the way they can be presented at the table. The meat is dark and rich, but by varying the method of cooking and the accompaniments, it need never become monotonous. Perhaps one of the most convenient ways to produce the meat, however, is in a terrine, which can be served whenever required, but is especially convenient for a shooting lunch in the open.

Terrine of Pigeons' Breasts

To make this terrine you require a large, medium-sized or small earthenware dish, according to the amount you want to make. Since it freezes well for several months, however, you may find it convenient to make a large amount at one time by using several small dishes. These can later be used up as and when required without any danger of waste.

For each dish you require enough pigeon breasts to fill it comfortably and a supply of fat bacon slices and sausage meat, or sage and onion stuffing, and a couple of bay leaves, as well as a good-sized glass of either brandy, sherry, or red wine.

Slice the pigeon breasts finely on a wooden board and season. Place a bay leaf in the bottom of the pie-dish, then line the inside and bottom with bacon. Cover this with a layer of sage and onion or sausage meat, then pigeon meat. Alternate the layers until the dish is full. Then press the whole mixture down hard to prevent any air holes forming and cover the top with bacon. Finally pour the glass of brandy, sherry or wine over the top and add the other bay leaf. Cover the whole dish with its lid or with aluminium foil, and put it in a water bath, 'en bain marie.' Place it in an oven set for around 300° F until the liquid in the terrine becomes clear, probably after a minimum of two hours, depending on the size of the pie-dish. Then leave it to cool and either use, or freeze, as required.

Pigeon Breasts in Creole Sauce

This is undoubtedly my favourite recipe. The ingredients for this are:

        1 lbs of pigeon breasts
        1 clove of garlic
        1 onion
        1 green pepper
        1 large tin of tomatoes; approx 14 oz:
        1 dessert spoon of capers
        1 tablespoon of tomato chutney
        1 teaspoon of soft brown sugar
        2 ozs of oil, or butter
        salt to taste
        Tabasco sauce ditto
        Lemon juice ditto
        10 black olives

With the ingredients to hand first slice the pigeon breasts in half lengthways and then crosswise into thin pieces. Peel and slice the onion thinly. Chop the pepper and capers. Fry the onion in oil until soft and transparent. Add the pigeon meat and increase heat until browned, stirring meanwhile. Add the garlic crushed, then the tomatoes and juice, followed by the pepper and capers, the brown sugar and the chutney. Season with salt. Then cover and cook gently over a low heat, or in a slow oven, until the pigeon is tender, approximately 15-20 minutes later. Meanwhile stone and halve the olives and add them to the dish, season to taste with the lemon juice and tabasco sauce. Then serve with rice or pasta and green salad. These ingredients should be enough for four.

Pigeon Pie

Probably one of the oldest country ways of producing pigeon is in a pie, and the breasts of young rooks can be mixed with pigeon breasts in this recipe, but only those of young rooks which have just left the nest, or they are inclined to taste bitter.

The ingredients required are:

Half a dozen pigeon breasts: from six pigeons:
Puff pastry
1 lb stewing steak
¼ lb streaky bacon
1 onion
2 hard boiled eggs
salt and pepper
seasoned flour
¾ pint of stock to fill the dish as required

Chop the steak into cubes, dice the bacon and chop the onion finely. Divide the eggs into slices. Roll the steak cubes in seasoned flour and stiffen with cooking oil. Place in the bottom of the pie dish and add the other ingredients in layers. Season and fill the dish with stock three-quarters full. Cover with the pastry, making a hole in the middle. Cook fast until the pastry has risen, then reduce the temperature and cook slowly until done. Add the remainder of the hot stock through the hole in the pie before serving. Enough for three or four people.

Roast Pigeon

One recipe which, surprisingly, seems to be left out of many books is roast pigeon, perhaps on the entirely false assumption that it is the commonest way of cooking pigeon, or that it is boring. Either of these assumptions is very far from the truth. Any game, and this goes for pigeons too, really well roasted with all the requisite trimmings of bread sauce, roast potatoes, brussels sprouts, peas or beans, and gravy is absolutely excellent. It can hardly be surpassed in any other form.

One or two per person:

> Bacon
> Orange slices
> Butter
> Mixed herbs
> Salt and Pepper

Stuff each bird with a lump of butter mixed with herbs and seasoning and a good thick slice of orange. Cover with bacon and truss. Cook at approximately 400°F in a fairly hot oven, basting frequently. Alternatively insert in a roastabag and cook at 370°F until done, removing the bacon towards the end to allow the birds to brown. If this is not done they will remain an unattractive pallid colour. Serve with a tomato sauce to which the gravy skimmed of its excess fat may be added.

Pigeon Casserole

One of the commoner ways of cooking pigeon, but none the less effective, is in a casserole. There are, of course, numerous ways of varying casseroles, but a good straightforward one is as follows:

4 pigeons
4 oz streaky bacon
12 small onions
4 oz butter
4 oz mushrooms
½ pint of stock
a large glass of red wine
2 sticks of celery
1 oz of raisins
bouquet garni: i.e. herbs such as parsley, thyme and bayleaf
redcurrant jelly as required

Truss the pigeons before cooking and dice the bacon, i.e chop it into small cubes. Melt half the butter in a pan and brown the bacon and then the pigeons. Add the wine and the stock as well as the bouquet garni, pepper and salt. Cover the casserole pan and leave to cook for two hours. Meanwhile fry the mushrooms and the onions, with the celery chopped into inch lengths, gently in the remainder of the butter. Add them to the casserole along with the raisins and cook for a further three-quarters of an hour. By this time the pigeons should be beautifully tender. Remove the casserole dish from the oven and extract the pigeons: Chop them in half and remove the string, then place on a warm serving plate with the vegetables. Add redcurrant jelly to the gravy. This makes an excellent accompaniment.

Curried Pigeon Breasts

If in doubt about how to cook your pigeons there is always a curry, and curried pigeon breasts are an excellent standby in the winter months. This can also be thoroughly recommended:

Curried Pigeon Breasts
1 lbs of pigeon breasts
2 cloves of garlic
1 large onion
1 pint of stock
1½ full tablespoons of full strength curry powder
3 oz dripping
half a lemon
2 bay leaves
1 tablespoon brown sugar
2 tablespoons tomato puree
Salt and black pepper to taste

Peel and chop finely both onion and garlic. Melt the dripping in a heavy pan and stir in one heaped tablespoonful of curry powder, fry over a low heat stirring gently for a full minute. Then add the chopped garlic and onion and fry a further two minutes. Pour in the stock and squeeze the juice from the half lemon into it. Add the bay leaves and bring to the boil. Then simmer over a low heat for three-quarters of an hour. Meanwhile chop the pigeon breasts in quarters. Season with salt and pepper and dust with the remaining curry powder. Then melt the rest of the dripping in a pan and fry the chopped pigeon breasts over a high heat for two or three minutes until browned. Add the curry stock and stir in the sugar and tomato puree. Then cover the pan with its lid and simmer the meat for about an hour and a half. By this time the stock should be reduced to a thick consistency and more curry powder can now be added after being lightly fried in a little dripping. It is best to leave the curry to cool and even better to leave it for two days or so before re-heating and serving with all the appropriate side dishes: I recommend sliced bananas, desiccated coconut, plenty of sweet mango chutney, raisins, chopped apple, chopped nuts and chopped melon in season.

All that is required is full use of the imagination and this infinitely adaptable bird can be eaten contentedly throughout the year.

Appendix

Table of the number of pellets per ounce of shot

Ozs. of shot	3	4	5	6	7	8
$1\frac{1}{2}$	210	255	330	405	510	675
$1\frac{7}{16}$	201	244	316	388	489	646
$1\frac{3}{8}$	192	234	303	371	468	618
$1\frac{5}{16}$	183	223	289	354	446	590
$1\frac{1}{4}$	175	213	275	338	425	563
$1\frac{3}{16}$	175	213	261	321	404	534
$1\frac{1}{8}$	157	191	248	304	383	506
$1\frac{1}{16}$	149	181	234	287	361	478
One	140	170	220	270	340	450
$\frac{15}{16}$	131	159	206	253	319	422
$\frac{7}{8}$	122	149	193	236	298	394
$\frac{13}{16}$	113	138	179	219	276	366
$\frac{3}{4}$	105	128	165	202	255	338
$\frac{11}{16}$	96	117	151	186	234	310
$\frac{5}{8}$	87	106	138	169	212	282
$\frac{9}{16}$	78	96	124	152	191	254
$\frac{1}{2}$	70	85	110	135	170	225

Bibliography

Richard Arnold *Pigeon Shooting* Faber, 1956. Kaye & Ward, 1979.

Max Baker *Sport with Woodpigeons* Shooting Times, 1934.

Archie Coats *Pigeon Shooting* Vista, 1963. Deutsch, 1972.

C.L.Coles *Shooting Pigeons* S.T.Library, 1963.

B.W.Dalrymple *Doves and Dove Shooting* Putnam, 1949.

Dennis G.Hogg *Know Your Woodpigeon Shooting* WAGBI, 1978.

John Humphreys *Modern Pigeon Shooting* Tideline, 1980.

A.E.B.Johnson *Shooting Wood-Pigeon* Jenkins, 1961. Boydell, 1980.

Dr R.K.Murton *The Wood Pigeon* Collins, 1963.

Come & Shoot Woodpigeons Game Conservancy, 1957.

Wildlife & Countryside Act : 1981.

Index

SPORT.